Praise for *Po*

It is comforting and encouraging
seriously, that rightly prioritizes t
that grounds the practice of pastoring in the words of Scripture.
This is a wonderful book from Jason Allen, and his talented team of
contributors, that will help equip the young pastor and encourage
the established pastor.

MICAH FRIES
Pastor of Brainerd Baptist Church

Talk about a book that's hard to put down; what pastor doesn't want to
be fully equipped? This book challenges, informs, and inspires.

JOHNNY HUNT
Pastor of Woodstock Baptist Church

As believers work together to push back lostness in North America and
around the world, no one—outside of Jesus—will play a more important
role than pastors. That's why this book is so critically important. It's
like sitting down with nine pastoral mentors who will talk frankly and
passionately with you about your most important pastoral roles as a
husband, father, preacher, evangelist, leader, and more. There is no
limit to what could happen if pastors lead the way in fulfilling the
Great Commission.

KEVIN EZELL
President of the North American Mission Board, SBC

In *Portraits of a Pastor*, we get a vision and pathway to more
faithful and fruitful pastoral ministry. I'm thankful for and challenged
by the content!

ED STETZER
Billy Graham Distinguished Chair, Wheaton College

Pastors have multiple roles. Each is demanding, indeed impossible
apart from the help of the Lord and the encouragement of the flock.
Apart from Jesus, a pastor can do nothing (cf. John 15:5). Since
1983, I have served as senior pastor at four different SBC churches—
each diverse in size. I understand something of the demands,
responsibilities, problems, and blessings of the pastorate. Pastors
need encouragement and sound, biblical advice to help them lead
their churches. That is why I recommend this new work, *Portraits
of a Pastor*. It will help every Christian understand more clearly the
responsibilities of a pastor, and why his role is so vital to the fulfillment
of the Great Commission.

STEVE GAINES
Senior Pastor, Bellevue Baptist Church, Memphis
President of the Southern Baptist Convention

The New Testament uses three rich words to designate the pastoral office and another twenty (at least) to define and describe pastoral duties. As a pastor and a professor, I often lament that books on pastoring fail to stand at the intersection of the academic and the practical and provide a full-orbed picture of the pastorate. Better than any book I have ever read, *Portraits of a Pastor* captures both the simplicity of the pastoral call and the complexity of the pastoral life. Until now, I've never seen a book daring and honest enough to render the mixture of head and heart, of cerebral and visceral, of a life occupied with the study of the Word and an obsession with reaching the lost, that serving as one of God's shepherds requires. Jason Allen and his colleagues instruct, but more importantly, they inspire. Reading this book made me grateful that I am a pastor, but it gave me the tools—and the way—to be a better one to the glory of God.

HERSHAEL W. YORK
Pastor of Buck Run Baptist Church in Frankfort, KY; Victor and Louise Lester Professor of Christian Preaching at The Southern Baptist Theological Seminary in Louisville, KY

The world at its worst needs the church at its best. Faithful churches require faithful pastors. Unfortunately, there are many who are confused about what the pastor is to be and do. *Portraits of a Pastor* paints a clear picture of the biblical role of the Christian pastor. Read this book!

H.B. CHARLES JR.
Pastor of Shiloh Metropolitan Tabernacle, Jacksonville, FL

This wise group of pastoral theologians has teamed up to provide church leaders with a valuable resource for local church ministry. *Portraits of a Pastor* will refresh weary ministry leaders and guide aspiring leaders. This is not corporate business principles baptized, but biblically rooted, Christ-exalting teaching. I was edified by it, and I pray that it will strengthen and build up Christ's church around the globe.

TONY MERIDA
Pastor, Imago Dei Church, Raleigh, NC

PORTRAITS OF A PASTOR

THE 9 ESSENTIAL ROLES OF A CHURCH LEADER

Jason Allen, General Editor

MOODY PUBLISHERS

CHICAGO

Edited by Matthew Boffey
Interior Design: Ragont Design
Cover Design: Erik M. Peterson
Cover photo by Liz Stack/MBTS

Library of Congress Cataloging-in-Publication Data

Names: Allen, Jason K., editor.
Title: Portraits of a pastor : the 9 essential roles of a church leader /
   Jason Allen, General editor.
Description: Chicago : Moody Publishers, [2017] | Includes bibliographical
   references.
Identifiers: LCCN 2017024073 (print) | LCCN 2017031446 (ebook) | ISBN
   9780802496232 | ISBN 9780802416346
Subjects: LCSH: Pastoral theology. | Christian leadership.
Classification: LCC BV4011.3 (ebook) | LCC BV4011.3 .P685 2017 (print) | DDC
   253--dc23
LC record available at https://lccn.loc.gov/2017024073

This book is dedicated, with deep appreciation, to the seven pastors who comprised the Presidential Search Committee and nominated me to be Midwestern Baptist Theological Seminary's fifth president in September of 2012. Under the leadership of the Holy Spirit, these men entrusted me with this most precious stewardship—one that I will forever cherish and for which I remain indebted to them.

Six of these men, Dwight Blankenship, Larry Dramann, Larry Lewis, Roger Marshall, Don Paxton, and Kevin Shrum, continue to serve the Lord as pastors and remain supporters of Midwestern Seminary.

The seventh man—to whom this book is most especially dedicated—served as chairman of the Presidential Search Committee. Now with the Lord in Heaven, Bill Bowyer's godliness, wisdom, and encouragement were essential to the search process and of inestimable encouragement to me personally.

Contents

Foreword

F or the church."

Those three words have become intrinsically tied to Jason Allen and the seminary he leads.

There is a good reason for the association.

Over the past several years, Dr. Allen has become a voice of incredible influence for churches and church leaders. His books, speaking platform, blog, and seminary are now vital and reliable sources of encouragement, information, advocacy, and direction for those who serve the bride of Christ. I have watched in amazement as his influence and contributions grow every day.

For the church.

If one is for the church, he must definitely be for the pastor. If the pastor is a good theologian, the church will be theologically sound. If the pastor is evangelistic, the church will be evangelistic. If the pastor is a great family man, the church will follow his example. If the pastor gives healthy attention to the preaching of God's Word, the church will be well-fed biblically.

You get the picture. Pastoral leadership is key. Pastoral leadership is vital.

Such is the reason *Portraits of a Pastor* is one of the most incredible books I have read "for the church." We are invited into the minds and hearts of nine of the most influential leaders in the church today. We are provided perspectives of pastoral leadership in a rich and powerful way. This book is the book that needs to be in the hands of pastors and those who love, follow, and support pastors. This book is already a timeless classic.

Over the course of a year, I have some level of contact or interaction with tens of thousands of pastors and other church leaders. There are those rare occasions where I let them know there is something that should be mandatory reading for their ministries, their leadership, and their personal lives. *Portraits of a Pastor* is one of those rare books.

Indeed, I feel so strongly about the content and contributors of this book that I have concluded it would be pastoral malpractice not to read it. Therefore, I will do my part to get it into the hands of every church leader I can.

For the church.

Thank you, Jason Allen, for this vital and timely book. Thank you to the other eight leaders who made such incredible and timeless contributions. Church leadership will be richer for it. Thus, our churches will be richer for it.

And now, to you, the readers: Read this book thoughtfully, carefully, and prayerfully. Ask how God can use each chapter to shape your ministries and your lives. Ask God to use this book for His glory through your leadership and through the churches you serve.

You see, "for the church" is not merely a slogan or a catchy phrase. It is a statement of why God chose us to lead. We are to be His leaders in His will in His churches for His glory, and *Portraits of a Pastor* will prove to be a poignant and powerful guide to that end.

It's just that good.

It is truly *for the church.*

THOM S. RAINER
President and CEO, LifeWay Christian Resources

Introduction

— Jason K. Allen —

Today's pastor wears many hats. Some of these hats are appropriate, aligning with the New Testament's expectations for the pastorate. Yet many are unhealthy, burdensome expectations imposed by the congregation—or even by the pastor himself.

In any case, the twenty-first-century pastorate can be a daunting position to hold. The biblical expectations are high, and the nonbiblical ones held by many churches are higher still. No pastor is omnicompetent, and none can be omnipresent. Yet today's pastor is often expected to be both.

In fact, some churches' expectations are so high—and stories of notoriously demanding churches are in strong supply—that many pastors experience burnout. A cottage industry has sprung up around this phenomenon: conferences, workshops, counselors, books, and materials all to support the beleaguered minister. Spoofs caricaturing the pastor's dilemma have arisen as well. Here's a common one:

After hundreds of fruitless years, a model minister has finally been found to suit everyone. It is completely guaranteed that he will please any church:

- He preaches only twenty minutes but thoroughly expounds the Word.
- He condemns sin but never hurts anyone's feelings.
- He works from 8:00 a.m. to 10:00 p.m. doing every type of work, from preaching in the pulpit to janitorial work.
- He makes one hundred dollars a week, wears good clothes, buys good books regularly, has a nice family, drives a nice car, and gives fifty dollars a week to the church.
- He stands ready to give to any good cause, also.
- His family is completely model in deportment, dress, and attitude.
- He is twenty-six years old and has been preaching for thirty years.
- He is tall, short, thin, heavyset, and handsome, has one brown eye and one blue eye, and parts his hair down the middle, left side dark and straight, right side blond and wavy.
- He has a burning desire to work with teenagers and spend all of his time with the older people.
- He smiles all the time with a straight face because he has a sense of humor that keeps him seriously dedicated to his work.
- He calls on church members fifteen times a day, spends all his time evangelizing the unchurched, and is never out of the office.

While this parody obviously overstates expectations, in some churches it may hit eerily close to home. During times of transition, churches often conduct congregational surveys to determine what to look for in their pastoral candidates. I've reviewed more than a few of these. The results are, much like this spoof, often somewhere between comical and maddening.

But what is the pastor to be? What must the pastor do? For these answers, we must turn to the Scriptures. That is the primary aim of this book. While you may find these essays challenging, my intent is for you to find them instructive and encouraging, not burdensome.

Within these pages, you'll find the pastorate presented in full color as we consider the pastor as shepherd, father, husband, preacher, theologian, church historian, evangelist, missionary, leader, and man of God. These chapters are both biblical and practical so that you might more faithfully, and more effectively, serve the local church.

Over the years, I have pastored several churches and served several others in various roles. Thankfully, my experiences have only included supportive, loving congregations. Now I find myself one step removed. I serve as a seminary president, where my responsibility and joy is to train ministers for church service. I consider my calling a high one, but only because I'm in the position of helping to prepare men for an even higher calling: pastoring a local church. It's a calling one should seek to fulfill with maximum faithfulness. May this book help you toward that noble, God-honoring end.

Pastor as Shepherd

— *Jared C. Wilson* —

I was almost forty years old before I knew what to "go out leaping like calves from the stall" meant (Mal. 4:2). This was because I was almost forty years old when I moved to pastor a small church in rural Vermont, where we lived across the street from a hilly cow pasture. We placed my writing table in the living room right under a big picture window that overlooked their grassy domain, and it was while looking out that window daydreaming that I actually saw calves leaping. I knew what that verse in Malachi meant before that moment, but at that moment I *really* knew.

I wonder if it would help many pastors today to spend some time with literal sheep. I know that ministry as shepherding is metaphorical, but our Lord chose that vocation for a reason. It's not an incidental metaphor. There must be some corollaries between a minister tending to his flock and a literal shepherd tending to his.

The title of my assigned "portrait" in this cooperative effort is rather interesting: "Pastor as Shepherd." The word *pastor* literally means "shepherd." So really, I am writing about the shepherd as shepherd! Or the pastor as pastor. On the surface, this may seem like an odd or rather obvious approach to describing the profile of a pastor. It is a bit like if you attended a parenting conference and encountered talks on fathers as fathers or mothers as mothers. It would almost not make sense.

But as you well know, today the evangelical church needs a reapprehension of the vocation of the pastor. What else can pastors be but pastors? As I learned in my initial training twenty-plus years ago, pastors can be teachers, coaches, "visionaries," and "catalytic agents of change." They can be leaders—even "thought leaders" (whatever that means). Pastors can be strategists, movement makers, marketers, innovators, and chief creative architects. But it seems almost accidental within the evangelical machinery to find a pastor who is actually *a pastor*. We have modernized ourselves beyond the resonance of the biblical image of a shepherd. The dominant vision of the vocation today has more to do with philosophies of leadership—which I've been told are thoroughly biblical, though I cannot find much written on the subject prior to the 1980s—and less to do with philosophies of livestock.

However, we ought to take God's chosen imagery for ministry seriously, and we encounter it in a striking way when Jesus restores Peter to ministry. There Jesus makes unequivocal the leader's commitment to care for the sheep. Specifically, there are three aspects of Peter's restoration that teach us about pastoring. I almost chose to clarify that these points refer to what *good* pastors do. But the more I thought about it, the more I realized, *No. These do not describe "good pastors"—they describe pastors, period.*

Brother pastor, if the following three statements are not true of you, it is not simply that you are not a good pastor; it means you are not pastoring. Here is an outline of the pastoral mandate:

1. Shepherds feed the sheep.
2. Shepherds love the Lamb.
3. Shepherds trust the Good Shepherd.

Our tendency to delineate between pastors and good pastors results, at least in part, from confusing *position* with *vocation*. We hand out the title "pastor" as if it may be divorced from the biblical expectations of shepherding. But my conviction, not born out of this passage alone but out of the greater biblical instruction on the pastoral office, is that these descriptions are the irreducible minimum of the pastoral vocation. In other words, your title may be pastor, your business card may say pastor, and your social media bio may say pastor, but if these three descriptions are not true of you, you are not a pastor. If you do not feed the sheep, love the Lamb, and trust the Good Shepherd, you are not a shepherd.

Let's now look at the passage at hand. Jesus has been betrayed, tortured, crucified, and resurrected. Hours before His ascension, He has this moment with one of his chief traitors. It is a moment as tender as it is powerful:

> When they had finished breakfast, Jesus said to Simon Peter, "Simon, son of John, do you love me more than these?" He said to him, "Yes, Lord; you know that I love you." He said to him, "Feed my lambs." He said to him a second time, "Simon, son of John, do you love me?" He said to him, "Yes, Lord; you know that I love you." He said to him, "Tend my sheep." He said to

him the third time, "Simon, son of John, do you love me?" Peter was grieved because he said to him the third time, "Do you love me?" and he said to him, "Lord, you know everything; you know that I love you." Jesus said to him, "Feed my sheep. Truly, truly, I say to you, when you were young, you used to dress yourself and walk wherever you wanted, but when you are old, you will stretch out your hands, and another will dress you and carry you where you do not want to go." (This he said to show by what kind of death he was to glorify God.) And after saying this he said to him, "Follow me." (John 21:15–19)

This, then, serves as the great pastoral commission, and it centers not on building a large ministry or casting a large vision. The central pastoral commission centers on our point number one: shepherds feed the sheep.

Shepherds Feed the Sheep

At the center of Peter's restoration is embedded not just a reality of identity but a reality of vocation. What I mean is, Jesus is not just reaffirming Peter's right standing with Himself; He is restoring Peter's pastoral office. He is giving him something to do, and it is the fundamental, essential, irreducible task of the shepherd: feed Christ's sheep.

Three times he commands him to care for the flock:

He said to him, "Feed my lambs." (v. 15)
He said to him, "Tend my sheep." (v. 16)
Jesus said to him, "Feed my sheep." (v. 17)

Allow me to speak briefly about one issue I believe central to the more recent debate about the sufficiency and reliability of the Bible in worship gatherings and in evangelism and apologetic conversations with unbelievers. I think if we trace back some of these pragmatic choices to the core philosophy driving them, we find in the attractional church, for instance, a few misunderstandings. The whole enterprise has begun with a wrong idea of what—biblically speaking—the worship gathering *is*, and even what *the church* is.

In some of these churches where it is difficult to find the Scriptures preached clearly and faithfully—as the reliable, authoritative, and transformative Word of God—we find that things have effectively been turned upside down. In 1 Corinthians 14, Paul uses the word "outsider" to describe unbelievers who are present in the worship gathering. He is making the case for our worship services to be intelligible, hospitable, and mindful of the unbelievers present, but his very use of the word "outsider" tells us that the Lord's-Day worship gathering is not meant to be primarily focused on the unbelieving visitor but on the believing saints gathered to exalt their King. In the attractional-church paradigm, this biblical understanding of the worship gathering is turned upside down. Consequently, mission and evangelism are actually inverted, because Christ's command to the church to "Go and tell" has been replaced by "Come and see."

Philosophically, many of these churches operate more like parachurches, and the result is that the sheep, the very lambs of God, basically become the outsiders. Thus you will have leading practitioners of these churches saying things like, "Church isn't for Christians—it's for outreach," or, "I never understand when someone claims they need to be fed—I don't see this in Scripture anywhere." This is troubling for a number of reasons, not least of which is that Jesus Himself affirmed the need. He told Peter, "Feed my sheep."

Interestingly, though, this "Come and see" approach can lead to sizeable growth. Many churches do exceptionally well at getting people into the pasture. However, they eventually discover that they are not doing so well at making sure the flock is nourished. In 2007, Willow Creek Community Church—showing commendable transparency—published the results of their REVEAL survey, an intensive and ruthlessly self-critical evaluation of their own success in growing fully devoted followers of Christ. A 2008 *Christianity Today* article explained the results this way:

> The study shows that while Willow has been successfully meeting the spiritual needs of those who describe themselves as "exploring Christianity" or "growing in Christ," it has been less successful at doing so with those who self-report as being "close to Christ" or "Christ-centered."[1]

While I respect Willow for their honesty and desire to minister more effectively, I do disagree with their solution, which is, "Our people need to learn to feed themselves through personal spiritual practices."[2]

Do maturing Christians need to take responsibility for their personal growth? Of course. Do they need to take ownership (as it were) of their spiritual disciplines? Absolutely. You are not saved or sanctified by somebody else's faith, and Paul even commands Christians to move on to maturity—to go from milk to meat, so to speak (see 1 Peter 2:2; Heb. 6:1; 1 Cor. 3:1–2).

But we have so much more to offer! In John 21, Jesus does not say to Peter, "Teach my sheep to self-feed." He says, "Feed my sheep." He says, "Tend my sheep."

If you are a pastor, honestly assess your preaching. When the saints gather on Sunday, what kind of food are you giving them? Are you loading them up with the bread of Christ? Are you ladling out the living water that quenches thirst forever?

Or are you loading them down with law? One of the many upside-down practices of some preachers today is how they aim messages of practical Christianity at non-Christians, handing out how-to guides on obedience to people whose hearts do not trust in Jesus. The best you can do with such a preaching strategy is create well-behaved unbelievers. Handing out how-to sermons is like commanding bricks without straw.

> *Lay out generously the new wine of salvation and the juicy meat of the glory of Jesus Christ. Let's send our people home fat with the gospel!*

Feed the sheep the gospel. The gospel is the only power of salvation—for the Jew and the Greek. Pastors, every week your people gather together starving. They are weary and worn-out, and for some it takes all the faith they have just to get through the door.

What is your job when they wander back into your pen on Sunday morning? Is it not to lay out the feast of the unsearchable riches of Christ? Is it not to present the true food of Christ and his matchless grace? They are hungry, brothers! They ask for bread. Do not give them stones! Lay out generously the new wine of salvation and the juicy meat of the glory of Jesus Christ. Let's send our people home *fat* with the gospel!

How you see your sheep will certainly affect how you feed them. If you see them as immature and unwilling to grow up, you will be inclined to withhold the food of the gospel from them. But if you see them as Jesus saw them—as harassed and helpless, like sheep without a shepherd—your compassion will move you to nourish them with the Word.

> *We need shepherds up to their elbows in Christ's little lambs. Pastor, if you do not get to the end of your week without at least a little wool on your jacket, you might not be a shepherd.*

Pastor, do you have compassion for your flock? It is something I find startlingly missing in so much ink spilled on philosophy of ministry. I listen to guys talk about their churches, and it has so much to do with strategy and technique and style and context—all important things—but sometimes I want to ask them, "Do you love your flock?"

Not every Christian man with an entrepreneurial spirit and a gift for speaking should be a pastor. I say this kindly—if your drive is not to feed the sheep, please quit. You may have missed your calling. Your gifts could be used more effectively elsewhere, perhaps for starting a business or a nonprofit.

We don't need any more salesmen in the pulpit. We need tenders of the sheep. We need shepherds up to their elbows in Christ's little lambs. Pastor, if you do not get to the end of your week without at least a little wool on your jacket, you might not be a shepherd.

Jonathan Edwards was fired from the pastorate at Northampton in June 1750. But they asked him to stay on and preach until they could find his replacement. Astonishingly, he agreed. How could he do this? I think we find a glimpse in his official farewell sermon, preached July 1, 1750 (one month after they had fired him):

I am not about to compare myself with the prophet Jeremiah, but in this respect I can say as he did, that "I have spoken the Word of God to you, unto the three and twentieth year, rising early and speaking." It was three and twenty years, the 15th day of last February, since I have labored in the work of the ministry, in the relation of a pastor to this church and congregation. And though my strength has been weakness, having always labored under great infirmity of body, besides my insufficiency for so great a charge in other respects, yet I have not spared my feeble strength, but have exerted it for the good of your souls. I can appeal to you as the apostle does to his hearers, Gal. 4:13, "Ye know how through infirmity of the flesh, I preached the Gospel unto you." I have spent the prime of my life and strength, in labors for your eternal welfare. . . .

I have tried all ways that I could think of tending to awaken your consciences, and make you sensible of the necessity of your improving your time, and being speedy in flying from the wrath to come, and thorough in the use of means for your escape and safety. I have diligently endeavored to find out and use the most powerful motives to persuade you to take care for your own welfare and salvation. I have not only endeavored to awaken you, that you might be moved with fear, but I have used my utmost endeavors to win you: I have sought out acceptable words, that if possible I might prevail upon you to forsake sin, and turn to God, and accept of Christ as your Savior and Lord. I have spent my strength very much in these things.[3]

Why would he accept their audacious request to keep preaching after they had fired him? Because he loved Christ's sheep and knew the sheep needed to be fed.

Shepherds love the sheep and feed the sheep.

They also love Jesus.

Shepherds Love the Lamb

Notice the connection Jesus makes in this dialogue. The love for the sheep is implicit, but feeding the sheep is explicitly connected to love for Jesus:

When they had finished breakfast, Jesus said to Simon Peter, "Simon, son of John, do you love me more than these?" (v. 15)

He said to him a second time, "Simon, son of John, do you love me?" (v. 16)

He said to him the third time, "Simon, son of John, do you love me?" (v. 17)

Some will point out the different Greek words here for love. Jesus is literally asking, "Do you *agape* me?" and Peter responds, "Yes, Lord, you know I *phileo* you." The inference is that Christ is asking about sacrificial love, and Peter is offering a "less-than" kind of love, more of a brotherly love. However, this alternation is insignificant. D. A. Carson, for instance, suggests that this is more a feature of John's style—that he is using the words inter-changeably, synonymously, which was fairly common even in other literature of the time.[4] And in any event, would it make sense for Peter, so tender in his repentance and desperate for Christ's approval, to offer him, even if insincerely, a *less-than* kind of love in this moment?

No, the exchange is well-translated simply in both cases as "love":

"Peter do you love me?"

"Yes, Lord, I love you."

The emphasis is not on the kind of love, but on the object of love. You won't feed the sheep unless you love the sheep, but you won't love the sheep truly until you love the Shepherd. Matthew 25 says:

> When the Son of Man comes in his glory, and all the angels with him, then he will sit on his glorious throne. Before him will be gathered all the nations, and he will separate people one from another as a shepherd separates the sheep from the goats. And he will place the sheep on his right, but the goats on the left. Then the King will say to those on his right, "Come, you who are blessed by my Father, inherit the kingdom prepared for you from the foundation of the world. For I was hungry and you gave me food, I was thirsty and you gave me drink, I was a stranger and you welcomed me, I was naked and you clothed me, I was sick and you visited me, I was in prison and you came to me." Then the righteous will answer him, saying, "Lord, when did we see you hungry and feed you, or thirsty and give

you drink? And when did we see you a stranger and welcome you, or naked and clothe you? And when did we see you sick or in prison and visit you?" And the King will answer them, "Truly, I say to you, as you did it to one of the least of these my brothers and sisters, you did it to me." (Matt. 25:31–40)

A neglect to love and tend to the sheep is a neglect to love and tend to the glory of Christ. Brothers, if you do not love Jesus, you are not pastoring.

What I notice a lot every day in the Christian spheres of social media is just how incredibly adept we evangelicals are at doctrinal criticism, cultural rebuke, theological analysis, biblical exegesis, apologetic and ethical debates, pithy spiritual *bon mots*, religious advice, and of course the use of quotations from Christian leaders present and past. But what seems less prevalent is love for Jesus.

When we see a Bible verse, we run its meaning through our minds and can expound on it with intelligence, but when we see Christ before us, we scarcely stagger at His beauty and exult in Him with awe.

When we see a lost person acting like a lost person in the news, our righteous indignation runs right through our fingertips to our keyboards, but when we see Christ before us, our righteousness ought to crumble, and we ought to run right to His feet in a posture of supplication and ask ourselves, "Do I love Jesus?"

When we see one of our Christian heroes saying something smart or funny or challenging, we send them a virtual high five and echo the proclamation in shouts of appreciation, but when we see Christ before us, do we lift Him high in our hearts and herald His glory with shouts of acclamation? Do we love Jesus?

I hear ministers and ministers-in-training talking about theology and technology all the livelong day, but it is frighteningly rare to walk away thinking, "Man, that guy loves Jesus." Even more frightening, I am increasingly burdened that people do not walk away from conversations with me having that same impression. I have committed the greatest of failures if I can turn a good phrase, preach a good sermon, explain good theology, give out good advice, and even articulate the good news, but people cannot genuinely say about me, "More than anything, it is clear that Jared loves Jesus."

Brothers, do you love the Lamb?

It will help you to remember this: your love for *Him* will never match His love for *you*. Your love, even if you mustered it all up in a moment of desperate self-abandonment, still could not match the love of His self-emptying, sacrificial blood offering for your sin to redeem you from death and hell.

This brings us, then, to our third and final point. When your care for the sheep is paltry and your love for the Lamb is spotty, at the very least we must know this: shepherds trust the Lord.

Shepherds Trust the Good Shepherd

While studying John 21 to write this chapter, I became convicted about something I had never realized. It's a familiar text, to be sure, but it occurred to me that John 21 should teach us to remove the word *never* from our vocabulary when we discuss the restoration of fallen pastors. After all, there is no greater moral failing than publicly denying Jesus Christ, especially in His hour of suffering.

Notice in the passage that Jesus is not just restoring Peter to relationship with Himself. He is not simply saying, "Peter, I believe you; I affirm your faith." He is restoring Peter to ministry: "Feed my sheep."

Why? Because while pastors must be biblically qualified, and while pastors must meet the high standards set forth for their office in 1 Timothy 3, Titus 1, and 1 Peter 5, the foundation of pastoral ministry is not based on your righteousness but on the righteousness of Christ.

John Calvin says, "Nothing was given to Peter through these words that is not also given to all the ministers of the Gospel."[5] I would add that there is nothing lacking in Peter in this moment that is not lacking in all ministers of the gospel.

It does not matter who you are, pastor. You may have the largest church in your city. You may have book deals. You may be on television and the radio. You may have a top-rated podcast. You may be the envy of every other pastor in your state. But compared to the Good Shepherd, and without the Good Shepherd, you are nothing.

To get the gravity of what is happening here, just think about all of the backstory embedded in this culminating exchange. Peter has followed Christ closely. He has been part of the inner circle within the inner circle. He has had his bright, shining moments. He has shown his inmost insecurity and outmost ignorance to the Lord. He has even, despite being warned about it, betrayed his Savior when put on the spot. So he comes to this moment (I imagine) with fear and trembling, full of angst and awkwardness, burdened under the weight of his sin.

We see it in verse 17: "He said to him the third time, 'Simon, son of John, do you love me?' *Peter was grieved* because he said to him the third time, 'Do you love me?'"

"Oh, please believe I love you!" Peter is saying, but really he is pleading, "Oh, please tell me you love me!" And this is the point of Jesus asking three times. It corresponds, of course, to Peter's three-time denial. As far as your sin may go, the grace of Christ goes further still. In this restoration, Jesus is saying to Peter, "You cannot out-sin my love for you."

Brother pastor, Jesus loves you. And it is this ludicrous grace that serves as your only sure foundation for pastoral ministry. I mean, just look at the context we find on either side of our focus text.

In John 21:5–6, we read, "Jesus said to them, 'Children, do you have any fish?' They answered him, 'No.' He said to them, 'Cast the net on the right side of the boat, and you will find some.'" *What?* That's a weird methodology. Is the water not connected underneath? It is not a different lake. But the logic did not matter. Why not? Verse 7 gives the reason: "It is the Lord!" Jesus had the power, and He was proving it to them in order to gain their trust.

Look at the other side of our focus passage: John 21:20–23. We read,

> Peter turned and saw the disciple whom Jesus loved following them, the one who also had leaned back against him during the supper and had said, "Lord, who is it that is going to betray you?" When Peter saw him, he said to Jesus, "Lord, what about this man?" Jesus said to him, "If it is my will that he remain until I come, what is that to you? You follow me!" So the saying spread abroad among the brothers that this disciple was not to die; yet Jesus did not say to him that he was not to die, but, "If it is my will that he remain until I come, what is that to you?"

Peter was concerned about the calling of another disciple. To this Jesus replied, "What's it to you? You follow me!" The same is true for us today.

"What about the pastor across the street?" we may ask.

"Let me worry about him. You follow me!" Jesus answers.

We play reputation games and compare ourselves to one another, but Jesus commands us to have our eyes on Him. We measure others to see how we stack up. We see the greener grass of another shepherd's pasture. We envy another pastor's numbers, his gifted team, his talented worship leader, his nicer facilities, his more successful ministry. Or, alternatively, we wonder when Jesus is going to get out there and "fix" all the other ministries that *aren't* as good as ours.

All the while, Jesus is bidding us to cast our gaze on Him: "What is all that to you?" He says. "You follow me."

In ministry, if you put your trust in anything but the Savior, you will always be disappointed anyway. I remember sitting in a counseling session with a couple on the verge of divorce. I had come with some of my fellow pastors—a last-ditch effort to plead for their reconciliation to each other. I instead found accusations, indictments of my own lack of care for them. The wife, hurt and bitter, said, "I needed my pastor."

The words just hung there. Nobody defended me. I could think of several things to say in my own defense—I *had* been there—but I swallowed them.

If you have been in ministry for any length of time, you have probably endured similar charges. Despite your best efforts, your imperfection is construed as neglect. People are looking for the Good Shepherd. As undershepherds, we fall short. And the sheep notice. They come in for silver bullets, and all we have is the cross.

Skills, gifts, wisdom, experience, strategies, intellect—all these things can adorn pastoral ministry, but the foundation of pastoral ministry must be faith in Christ Jesus alone. *His* goodness, *His* wisdom, *His* power.

But what if I am not successful? What if I don't even have *the gifts and the growing ministry that might tempt me into idolatry?* I think our passage speaks to that:

> Truly, truly, I say to you, when you were young, you used to dress yourself and walk wherever you wanted, but when you are old, you will stretch out your hands, and another will dress you and carry you where you do not want to go." (This he said to show by what kind of death he was to glorify God.) And after saying this he said to him, "Follow me." (John 21:18–19)

Jesus promised Peter that the ministry would be costly and that it would take him where he wouldn't want to go. Should we expect anything less for ourselves?

Yet note that even the death of Peter was precious to Jesus ("This he said to show by what kind of death he was *to glorify God"*). God cares about our ministries.

If you have children, do you remember when they were little and would bring you some token of their immature affection? I think of my daughters, who would come in from playing in the yard clutching a little bit of greenery in their chubby fists. They might pull up a dandelion or a clump of grass. It could be a weed. But they bring it in as a flower, presenting it gleefully as a present to their mother or me.

What do you do with such a gift? Why, you treat it like it is the most precious rose to be found, do you not? You take that grass or weed, put it in a vase, fill it with water, and set it up on the counter. In the same way, the Father accepts and adorns your ministry as sons through Christ.

So even if the call of the pastor is to die, we trust the Good Shepherd. And we follow the Good Shepherd, who lays down His life for the sheep.

You have no other foundation, nothing else in which to put your trust. It doesn't even matter how gospel-centered your ministry philosophy is—if your heart is not gospel-centered, you have *nothing*. Your ministry, your platform, your very body itself winds down, wears out, fades away, and dissolves. Only God's glory will remain.

So where will you put your trust? Trust the Shepherd, brother. You have no other foundation. Let us declare, with all our weary confidence, our trust in the Savior, using the words of the old hymn:

> My hope is built on nothing less
> Than Jesus' blood and righteousness.
> I dare not trust the sweetest frame,
> But wholly trust in Jesus' name.
> On Christ the solid rock I stand,
> All other ground is sinking sand.
> All other ground is sinking sand.[6]

Pastor as Husband and Father

— *Daniel L. Akin* —

I believe two of God's greatest gifts this side of heaven are marriage and family. I believe they are good gifts from a great God. My wife, Charlotte, and I have been married since 1978, and we have deeply enjoyed our years together. We have had our good days and our bad days, like every couple, but our life together has truly been a blessing from the Lord. We were also graced by God with four sons, each now serving in ministry. We have three beautiful daughters-in-law (as of 2017) and a growing quiver of grandchildren. We totally agree with the psalmist: "Sons are indeed a heritage from the LORD, children, a reward. Like arrows in the hand of a warrior are the sons born in one's youth. Happy is the man who has filled his quiver with them. Such men will never be put to shame when they speak with their enemies at the city gate" (Ps. 127:3–5 HCSB).

Tragically, we live in a fallen and broken world, where many are not experiencing what God designed for marriage and family. Unfortunately, this is all too common in the homes of ministers who seek to lead and guide the churches of Jesus. Sin and confusion rob them of the delights and joys God planned for this sacred covenant relationship. Marital disharmony, fractured families, and broken lives are all around us. This is not how it should be.

When the Bible addresses God's expectations of anyone who leads His churches, two things are crystal clear. *First*, if married, he must be a man who is devoted to his wife. *Secondly*, if a father, he must be a man who is committed to his children.

Of course, some pastors may be unmarried or childless. Nothing in the text of Scripture suggests this disqualifies them from ministry. Pastors do not lead and serve based solely on their own experiences, but on the authority and wisdom that is grounded in God's Word. While on certain occasions a single pastor may need to lean on others in the church who are married and have children, most of his ministry will certainly be *shaped* but not *hindered* by his experience as one who is unmarried.

At the same time, there is a sense in which the single pastor must still be devoted to his family. First, he can and must live with an integrity and intentionality that will be a blessing to any future family he may have. Additionally, he ought to live with this same integrity and intentionality among the family the Lord has called him to serve—his church family. He can love the families around him, encourage singles, learn from parents and grandparents, and help support marriages and raise children in the context of the body of Christ. All of this can be done in service to the Lord and with an eye toward potential future relationships. In other words, a single pastor can still be a "family man" in a very real sense! Hopefully this chapter is equally beneficial in that regard.

Coming back to a married pastor's responsibility toward his family, Paul says in 1 Timothy 3:2 (HCSB), "An overseer, therefore, must be above reproach, the husband of one wife" (cf. Titus 1:6). Literally, he is to be a "one-wife husband." Concerning his children, this is made plain where we see he must be "one who manages his own household competently, having his children under control with all dignity. (If anyone does not know how to manage his own household, how will he take care of God's church?)" (1 Tim. 3:4–5 HCSB). Again, in Titus 1:6, a parallel account, Paul says that an elder is to have "faithful children not accused of wildness or rebellion" (HCSB). The particulars of what this looks like are set forth most clearly in Ephesians 5:25–6:4. However, before we walk through those verses and make specific applications, it is helpful and instructive to provide a wider biblical context. Doing so shows us what God planned, what went wrong, and how to regain something of the "paradise lost" in our homes.

Overview of the Bible on Marriage and Family

The three great movements and their respective texts can be outlined as follows:

CREATION	→	FALL	→	REDEMPTION
Genesis 1–2		Genesis 3–4		Ephesians 5–6
equal image bearers		"battle of the sexes" and family discord		a redeemed and restored marriage and family

There is a remarkable redemptive biblical storyline when it comes to marriage and the family. While this list is not exhaustive, it does note the major biblical texts that stretch from creation to new creation:

GENESIS 1:26–28

God creates humanity as male and female and commissions them, together, to fill the earth with His image bearers.

↓

GENESIS 2:18–25

From the first man, God creates the first woman and gives her to the man as a helper who complements him as a suitable companion.

↓

DEUTERONOMY 6:1–9

God charges His covenant people, Israel, to submit to and obey His loving commands, and to pass those commands on from generation to generation. The primary context of this generational transmission was to be the family.

↓

RUTH

God uses the kinsman-redeemer Boaz to preserve the family line that would produce Israel's greatest king (David) and only Messiah (Jesus).

↓

PSALMS 127–128

Children are a blessing from the Lord to be treasured and cherished, even while the family's ultimate success depends on God's gracious care.

↓

PROVERBS 31:10–31

The godly wife is to be praised for her strong character, her hard work, her wise words, and her deep faith.

↓

SONG OF SOLOMON

The Song extols the glories of marital intimacy and points to the pure love that Christ has for the church.

↓

1 CORINTHIANS 7:1–40	Marriage is affirmed as a legitimate decision for those Christians who want to pursue Christ in holiness. At the same time, marriage is not ultimate and may be bypassed for the sake of serving Christ unhindered.
↓	
EPHESIANS 5:21–6:4	Marriage is meant to point to Christ's relationship with His church, for whom He died. The Christian family is meant to be founded and centered on the gospel.
↓	
COLOSSIANS 3:18–21	For the Christian, marriage and family are meant to be "in the Lord"—in all things submitted to the lordship of Christ.
↓	
1 PETER 2:13–3:7	Men and women should seek, above all, to honor the Lord in their marriages.
↓	
REVELATION 21:2–9	The fulfillment of marriage will come when Christ returns for His bride, the church, and establishes new heavens and a new earth where He will dwell with His people forever.

The picture of a godly family that Scripture puts forth is one where husbands care for their wives, wives for their husbands, and parents for their children, raising them in the fear of the Lord and the knowledge of Scripture—all centered on and reflecting the gospel. And while there are plenty of places in Scripture one could go to talk specifically about a godly man's responsibility to his family, Ephesians 5:25–6:4 is paramount among them.

Ephesians 5:25–6:4 grounds family roles in the redemptive work of Christ. For a husband, his posture is to mirror that of Jesus, specifically His atoning and sacrificial death. Just as Christ laid His life down for the sake of His bride, the church, so the husband should lay his life down for the sake of his wife. He puts her needs above his own. His concern is for her protection, growth, and flourishing. His desire is for her sanctification. All of this finds its archetype in Jesus Himself.

When the godly man turns to his children, he likewise works for their good. He does this by raising them "in the Lord" (6:1). The wisdom he offers and the instruction he gives should be that which comes from God Himself (6:4), ultimately pointing to their need for salvation and its provision in Christ.

Now that we have a broad overview of a godly man's responsibilities to his family, what are the specific instructions Paul sets forth? And what does it mean for the pastor, as a man of God, to be a family man? In this chapter we'll move from broad principles to pastor-specific application, especially given that a pastor's family lives a unique existence.

A Pastor Will Love His Wife

Male-bashing has been a favorite American sport for some time now. It is epitomized by a cover story in *Time* magazine some years ago, which displays the body of a man with the head of a pig. The lead story for that Valentine's edition of the magazine was entitled, "Men: Are They Really That Bad?" The gist of the article was, "Yes, they are." Give them your heart, and they will break it. Put your trust in them, and they will let you down. Count on them, and they too often won't even show up.[1]

I think it must be admitted that men have too often invited such ridicule and scorn. Too many males have failed to act like men. They have come up short as husbands and fathers. This is sometimes true even for pastors who say one thing from the pulpit while doing something entirely different in their own homes. However, this is where a daily, intimate relationship with Jesus

Christ makes all the difference. A redeemed man cannot be satisfied with a halfhearted devotion to his wife and children. Christ in him compels more. Christ in him demands more. Divine expectations are laid upon him that he cannot and will not ignore.

In Ephesians 5:25–33, the Bible teaches that a godly, Spirit-filled husband will *love* his wife. Paul uses the Greek word *agape*, a word that occurs six times in Ephesians 5:25–33. Its first appearance in verse 25 is a present imperative, which means it is not a request or a suggestion, but a binding command. A man is *commanded* by God to continually and consistently love his wife. Not leaving the idea of love to our imagination, Paul develops five facets of the Christlike love every husband is to demonstrate toward his wife.

The man of God's love should be sacrificial (v. 25)

A husband is to love his wife just at Christ "loved the church and gave Himself for her" (HCSB). Paul grounds his theology of marriage in the atonement, in the *cross*. The emphasis of the love described here is volitional more than emotional. This love is a choice, a decision, an act of the will. This is not an "I love you if . . ." or an "I love you because . . ." No, this is an "I love you anyway. I love you even when you may not be lovely." This is how Jesus loved us when we were dead in sin (Eph. 2:1–10) and alienated from God (Eph. 2:11–22). He loved us when we were not lovely. He loved us in spite of our rebellion and rejection of Him. He gave Himself away in death for the good of others—what we might describe as "passion in action." Emotional feelings have their proper place in marriage. They are usually that which gets us started in a relationship. However, they cannot sustain us for a lifetime. We need something wider and deeper. We need a sacrificial love that flows out of the sacrificial love of Christ for us—a love that seeks the best for another, even at great cost to oneself.

The man of God's love should be sanctifying (vv. 26–27)

Christ gave Himself for His church "to make her holy, cleansing her with the washing of water by the word. He did this to present the church to Himself in splendor, without spot or wrinkle or anything like that, but holy and blameless" (HCSB). The truth of this text, as it relates to Christ and the church, is readily apparent. But how does it apply to the husband-wife relationship? I believe it works like this: because a wife is married to a godly husband, she is both encouraged and enabled to grow in Christlikeness. The husband is her helper in the process of sanctification, in her being conformed to the image and likeness of Jesus. This means a husband will shepherd his wife. He will lead and guide her to maturity as a radiant woman of God. He will help her and not hinder her in her pursuit and passion for the things of God.

Let me raise a much neglected question in this context: men, are you committed to making your wife a success? I know that may seem like an unusual question, and one that may not fit our normal male categories of thinking. However, it should when rightly understood. Are you committed to making your wife a success, not in man's eyes, but in God's? Have you determined that if you only shepherd one person in your entire ministry, it will be your wife? Then your children? Do you understand that shepherding begins in the home?

The man of God's love should be sensitive (v. 28)

Ephesians 5:28 says, "Husbands ought [there is a moral imperative here] also to love their own wives [it is exclusive] as their own bodies; he who loves his wife loves himself" (my translation). A husband naturally is sensitive to himself. He pays close and careful attention to himself. He knows when he is having a good day or a bad day. He knows when he is up or down, happy or sad, mad or glad. In the same way, he should be sensitive and aware of what is going on in the life of his wife. He needs to develop what I call a "marital radar system" that picks up signals that come from his wife. I should be quick to add that this radar system should—it must!—improve with practice and age. The way she walks into the room, her body language, her facial expression, and the tone of her voice are just a few of the areas a wise and godly husband will study and learn to read. He will certainly find this a challenge, but he will pursue it diligently because it is what His Lord has done and continues to do for him.

The man of God's love should be satisfying (vv. 29–30)

Paul says a wife should be "nourished" and "cherished" by her husband's love. Both of these words are present participles, indicating continuous action. A husband continually nourishes or feeds his wife with his love, and he continually cherishes or honors her with that same love. His love strengthens and sustains her. His love informs her that there is a place in his heart reserved just for her. She knows and understands that outside of Jesus, no one is more important to him than she. She trusts this man. She can rest and be confident in his love.

The man of God's love should be specific (vv. 31–33)

Paul not only grounds his theology of marriage in the atonement, but in the doctrine of creation, too. Verse 31 is a direct quote of Genesis 2:24 (note Jesus' citation of this as well in Matt. 19:5). The original context is before the fall in Genesis 3. This is important to note, as it informs the entire context of Ephesians 5:21–33. In verse 33, Paul concludes by charging the husband—having left father and mother to join or cleave to his wife—to "let each one of you in particular so love his own wife as himself" (NKJV). God calls a husband to be a "one woman kind of man." He calls him to love his wife in such a way that she knows, the children know, friends know, and even his enemies know, that this man is in love with and devoted to only one woman, and that woman is his wife. This man is neither a flirt nor a fool. He commits to being alone with one woman and only one woman, and that woman is his wife. And, knowing that even the best of men can be led astray, he constantly reminds himself that it does not matter how much he loves Jesus or his wife, the wrong person + the wrong place + the wrong time = the wrong thing happening. The tragic example of King David, a man after God's own heart, is never far from his mind (see 2 Sam. 11).

What Does It Look Like?

So what does a marriage look like when a man loves his wife in this fivefold manner? How can he bless her, day in and day out, as he comes to more fully love and understand her? I believe a husband can be a blessing to his wife by loving her as Christ loved the church and by giving her specific gifts of love that speak directly to her heart as a woman. What do these gifts look like? I suggest seven that I believe find warrant throughout the divine revelation.

Be a spiritual leader

Be a man of God with courage, conviction, commitment, compassion, and character. Take the initiative in cultivating a spiritual environment for the family. Live out faithfully and consistently, before all, a life founded on the Word of God. Lead your wife in becoming a woman of God, and take the lead in training the children in the things of the Lord (Ps. 1; Eph. 5:23–27; 6:1–4). Don't let the only people you study the Bible with in a given week be your elders or the leaders you're discipling. Study with your wife. Pray with your wife. Confess sins with your wife. Be one in your spiritual development. Your wife should not be a stranger to your spiritual leadership, but rather the first to benefit from it.

Give her personal affirmation and appreciation

Praise her for her personal attributes and qualities. Praise her virtues as a wife, mother, and homemaker. Openly commend her, in the presence of others, as a marvelous mate, friend, lover, and companion. It is even appropriate to praise your wife from the pulpit, in moderation. Help her feel that no one is more important in this world to you but King Jesus (Prov. 31:28–29; Song of Sol. 4:1–7; 6:4–9; 7:1–9). This means you must be around enough to see and affirm her qualities, gifts, and contributions to your marriage and family. You must take time to notice and make the effort to affirm. Don't let the ministry sideline this crucial responsibility. Your wife needs your love.

Show personal affection (romance her)

Shower her with timely and generous displays of affection. Romance her in a language she understands! Tell her and show her how much you care for her with a steady flow of words, cards, flowers, gifts, and common courtesies. Remember, affection is the environment in which sexual union is more often enjoyed and a wonderful marriage develops (Song of Sol. 7:10–13; Eph. 5:28–29,

33). These efforts are especially meaningful when ministry is most demanding. If your wife knows you are carrying heavy ministry weights but are going above and beyond to communicate love to her, she'll know undoubtedly that you prioritize her. Pastor, if you're in such a season, put something on your calendar right now and treat it like your most important commitment—because it is.

Initiate intimate conversation

Talk with her at the feeling level (heart-to-heart). Listen to her thoughts about the events of her day with sensitivity, interest, and concern. Such conversations with her convey a desire to understand her, not change her (Song of Sol. 2:8–14; 8:13–14; 1 Peter 3:7). As a pastor, you are used to giving counsel and "fixing things." Put that impulse away with your wife until she asks for it, and instead practice listening and empathy.

Always be honest and open

Look into her eyes and, in love, always be truthful (Eph. 4:15). Explain your plans and actions clearly and completely, because you are responsible for her and the children. Lead her to trust you and feel secure with you. I do not think a pastor must or even *should* share all the details of his ministry with his wife, especially when it comes to sensitive counseling situations. At the same time, you ought never to be deceptive or secretive toward her. In every case you must be truthful. In most cases, you can be somewhat specific, even if you cannot provide many details.

Provide home support and stability

Take hold of the responsibility to house, feed, and clothe the family. Provide and protect, and do not feel sorry for yourself when things in the ministry and life get tough. Look for concrete ways to improve home life. Raise the marriage and family to a safe and more fulfilling level. Remember, the husband/father is the security hub of the family (1 Tim. 5:8). This will look different in every family, but you must resist the temptation to only work at the office and only rest while at home. Be an equal partner when it comes to caring for the home, doing chores, and helping the children with homework. Actively seek to create a healthy and trusting family culture by talking with your kids, together and individually. Give your wife time to rest, relax, and even get away by herself for a while. All of this will enhance the health and stability of your home and family life.

> *Remember that at the end of the day you come home to your own flesh. Should the doors of your church ever close—or, God forbid, you get booted out—there is still one person who will be by your side. Love that woman.*

Demonstrate family commitment

By now you get the sense that a faithful pastor prioritizes his wife and kids, but the point bears repeating. After the Lord Jesus, put your wife and family first. Commit the necessary time and energy to spiritual, moral, and intellectual development of the children. For example, pray with them (especially at night by the bedside) and read the Bible and good Christian books to them. Engage in sports with them. Just spend time with them. Do not play the fools' game of working long hours trying to get ahead while your children and spouse languish in neglect (Eph. 6:4; Col. 3:19–20).

The man of God is to love his wife in biblical, tangible, and practical ways. Pastor, remember the wife of your youth. Remember that at the end of the day you come home to your own flesh. Should the doors of your church ever close—or, God forbid, you get booted out—there is still one person who will be by your side. Love that woman. Enjoy the gift of marriage. Cherish your wife. Stoke whatever embers are growing cold, and warm yourself by the fire of gospel love. It will be a delight to your soul and hers and will energize both of you as you labor together in the Lord.

In fitting order, Paul instructs husbands in Ephesians 5:23–31 before instructing fathers in Ephesians 6:1–4. After giving attention to his own marriage, a pastor must give attention to his children.

A Pastor Will Train Up His Children

On April 26, 1989, the "Queen of Comedy" Lucille Ball passed away. Sometime before her death she was interviewed on television by talk-show host Merv Griffin, who asked Lucy some very interesting and important questions: "Lucille, you've lived a long time on this earth and you are a wise person. What's happened to our country? What's wrong with our children? Why are our families falling apart? What's missing?"

To those series of questions Lucy quickly responded and said, "Papa's missing. Things are falling apart because Papa's gone. If Papa were here, he would fix it."[2]

Lucy was right. In 1960, only 8 percent of children in America lived without daddy in the home. In 2012, that number was over 24 percent. Almost 50 percent of African American children live with only their mothers at home. Yes, in too many homes Papa is gone.[3]

And yet, there is another tragedy that stalks our land and comes alongside this one, a tragedy that often afflicts the home of Christian ministers. There are homes where dad is present physically, but not personally and emotionally. He is not really there. He is tuned out, checked out, and clueless about what is going on in the lives of his children. He does not know his children.

I think the sorrow and heartbreak experienced by far too many children is expressed well in a letter written to *Seventeen* magazine years ago. Listen to what this teenage girl said for all the world to hear about her relationship with her daddy:

> Have you ever heard of a father who won't talk to his daughter? My father doesn't seem to know I'm alive. In my whole life, he has never said he loves me or given me a goodnight kiss unless I asked him to. I think the reason he ignores me is because I'm so boring. I look at my friends and think, "If I were funny like Jill or a super brain like Sandy or even outrageous and punk like Tasha, he would put down his paper and be fascinated." I play the recorder, and for the past three years I've been a soloist in the fall concert at school. Mom comes to the concerts, but Dad never does. This year, I'm a senior, so it's his last chance. I'd give anything to look out into the audience and see him there. But who am I kidding? It will never happen.[4]

Knowing your mom and dad care, and knowing they will be there when you need them, can sometimes be the difference between life and death for a child.

I read a story in *Focus on the Family*'s monthly magazine several years ago that had run earlier in *Reader's Digest*. It is one of the most powerful stories I have ever read concerning the difference the love of a daddy made in the life of one of his children:

> One day, a father took his two elementary school-age children for a ride in a pontoon boat. They were traveling down the river when suddenly the motor stopped. When the father looked behind him, he noticed something familiar about the red sweater tangled up in the propeller. Then his young son yelled, "Sherry fell in!" In horror, the father saw his little girl entwined in the propeller of the boat. She was submerged just beneath the surface of the water, looking straight into the eyes of her daddy and holding her breath. He jumped into the water and tried to pull the motor up, but the heavy engine wouldn't budge. Time was running out. Desperately, the father filled his own lungs with air and dipped below the surface, blowing air into his daughter's lungs. After giving her air three times, the father took a knife from his shocked son's hand. He quickly cut the red sweater from the propeller and lifted his daughter into the boat. Although she had survived, her deep cuts and bruises needed medical attention, so they rushed her to the hospital. When the crisis was over, the doctors and nurses asked the girl, "How come you didn't panic?" "Well, we've grown up on the river and my dad always taught us that if you panic, you die. And besides, I knew my daddy would come and get me."[5]

Do your children know beyond a shadow of a doubt that you would come and get them, no matter what? If your son was arrested for underage drinking, would you go pick him up from the local jail? If your daughter was caught in an immoral relationship, does she know that she would still be welcome at the family dinner table? If your high schooler started questioning the faith you've taught him so faithfully and so consistently, would he know that you were a safe person to whom he could ask his questions?

Ephesians 6:1–4 provides a simple, basic strategy for loving and training our children. Two guiding principles are put before us—principles that are directly applied to the man of God: he will *educate* and *encourage* his children.

The man of God educates his children (6:1–3)

A good father will teach his children that God expects them to obey their parents. "Obey" is a present imperative and word of command. God does not ask or suggest. He commands children, as an act of obedience to Him, that they obey their father and mother. He then qualifies the statement in two ways. First, He says it is "in the Lord." Second, He says, "for this is right." In the context, I believe "in the Lord" means something like "unto the Lord" (HCSB: "as you would the Lord"). In other words, a good father (and the same goes for mothers) will teach his children that when they are obeying dad and mom, they are obeying Jesus. As Charlotte and I raised and trained our boys, we tried to help them understand that their obedience or disobedience was not ultimately toward us, but toward the Lord. When they obeyed us, they were obeying Jesus. It is "in the Lord." It is also "right." This is the way that God has designed and structured the home. This is His ordained pattern.

However—and this is very important—good parents don't just tell their children what to do. They also help them understand why. Why should they "obey" (v. 1) and "honor" (v. 2) their father and mother? Paul, being the theologian that he is, grounds this admonition in Old Testament Scripture, specifically the fifth of the Ten Commandments found both in Exodus 20:12 and Deuteronomy 5:16. God provides a twofold promise to children who obey and honor their father and mother. The promises attached to obedience to these commands are (1) a better life ("that it may go well with you") and (2) a longer life ("that your days may be long in the land"). God establishes a general covenant with children, promising His blessings when they obey and honor their parents. Children need to be taught by their parents these wonderful promises from the God who loves them and only wants what is best for them.

The man of God encourages his children (6:4)

Verse four is directly addressed to fathers and is rooted in Deuteronomy 6:1–9, especially verses 4–9. It is interesting to note verses 2–3 draw from Deuteronomy 5 and verse 4 from Deuteronomy 6.

Fathers in particular (though I don't think mothers are excluded from these verses) are given a negative and a positive command. Negatively, they are not to provoke their children to anger. Fathers should be careful to not be unnecessarily harsh or dictatorial with their children. The parallel account in Colossians 3:21 is helpful: "Fathers, do not embitter your children, or they will become discouraged" (NIV). Fathers are not to be frustrated drill sergeants or CEOs always barking out orders to their children. There is no hopeful future in such an approach. In contrast, fathers should "bring them up [or 'nourish them'; same Greek word translated 'nourish' in Eph. 5:29] in the training and instruction of the Lord" (HCSB). Eugene Peterson, in *The Message*, paraphrases it, "Take them by the hand and lead them in the way of the Master."

Now, some parents get frustrated in this parental assignment because they draw a faulty conclusion. "Children don't listen to mom and dad," they say. The experts tell us they are more influenced by *peer pressure* than *parental guidance*. However, the experts are wrong. *Newsweek* magazine once noted, "In a recent national poll, teenagers named their parents as their No. 1 heroes."[6] When asked what they would most like to have with them if stranded on a deserted island, the number one answer of Gen Xers was, "My parents." The other requested items were music (24 percent), a computer (21 percent), books (15 percent), and a television (10 percent).[7] No, the fact is, your children do care what you *think*, they do listen to what you *say*, and they pay a whole lot of attention to what you *do*.

What Does It Look Like?

So, returning once more to the arena of practical theology, what are some principles or guidelines that can inform our parenting as we seek to train up our children "in the way of the Master"? Here are ten quick ideas for your consideration:

Seek to see life from their perspective

I call this "incarnational parenting." God entered our world through His Son (John 1:14; Phil. 2:6–8) and showed us He loves us. Get into the world of your children. Try to consider their age, maturity, interests, and challenges. Gain their viewpoint about what is going on. Doing this is easier said than done, but it is essential nevertheless. Taking the time to do this is critical if you're a pastor. How many pastors' kids grew up to say something

How many pastors' kids grew up to say something like, "I know Dad loved me, but it seems like he loved the church more"? Don't let it be so of you.

like, "I know Dad loved me, but it seems like he loved the church more"? Don't let it be so of you. Taking time to enter into the world of your child—in ways that are natural and meaningful to them—communicates that they are your most precious sheep.

Work at being a good partner

Good partners almost always make good parents. Seeing mom and dad love each other (1) brings security into the world of a child and (2) models for them a healthy marriage. This can be as simple as letting your children see you and your spouse problem-solve together. Life is difficult, and so is marriage. Let them see you tackle it together! The same could be said of ministry. When possible and wise, evangelize, counsel, and show hospitality together. This will surely strengthen your marriage and serve your children.

Lovingly discipline them

In our family, we tried to provide a big playing field, not a small one. Why? Because kids are kids, and if the box is too small, they will break the rules constantly and you will probably be inconsistent in your discipline. We always told our four sons they would establish the size of the playing field. If they were faithful, truthful, and trustworthy, the playing field would get bigger and bigger. If they were unfaithful, untruthful, and untrustworthy, the playing field would get smaller and smaller.

We also adjusted the way we disciplined as they grew older. We believe spanking, in moderation and always under control, is both biblical and effective when the children are small (see Prov. 29:15). However, as they grow older, unless the situation is extreme and exceptional, rebuke and restriction are more effective ways to mold and shape their character and behavior. This is the goal of discipline—to train them to fear God and walk faithfully before Him. The pastor, therefore, must take care not to discipline his children for embarrassing him or not fitting the mold of the perfect pastor's family. These attitudes reveal a prideful and selfish heart rather than a caring and loving one.

Love them with your eyes and words

Understand the power of both the eyes and the tongue (see Prov. 20:12 and James 1:19). With a look of the eye, we can build up or tear down, communicate love or contempt. Words, of course, are powerful weapons. They can bless or curse. Parents will often say things to their child that they would never say to a stranger—and seldom even to a dog. We all fail far too often in this area, and it is something we must constantly watch. To serve as a pastor is to work with words, which means you will have plenty of practice using yours to influence people, either for good or ill. When it comes to those over whom you have the greatest influence—your children—use that practice to communicate love and affection.

Learn that love is a beautiful four-letter word sometimes best spelled T.I.M.E.

Work hard to be at important events in the lives of your children. Go to football and basketball games, concerts, and plays, and get them on the calendar at the earliest possible date. Be faithful not to let anything replace them. When our oldest sons were seniors in high school, our four boys played more than seventy basketball games combined! We saw almost all of them, and our boys more than once told us how much it meant to them.

Pastors face untold demands for their time and attention, more than many church members understand or acknowledge.

The decision to protect time with their children is made all the more difficult by the fact that pastoral responsibilities are almost always *good* things that could easily justify the extra time. But let me encourage you never to let the good things of pastoral ministry cost you the *best* thing—your children. Inevitably there will be times when your wife and kids have to make sacrifices, but the general pattern of your ministry should be one of protecting time with your family. You will not regret it.

Make it a habit to hold, hug, and kiss your children

Love by touch takes different shapes and forms through the years, but it should always be a healthy and vital part of family life. Remember Ecclesiastes 3:5: there is "a time to embrace." With our children, anytime is a good time. As a pastor, your children will see you care for and embrace many who are suffering. Make sure you show them the same tenderness and affection.

Make your home a fun place to be

Making your home a fun one, a place where the children will be glad to bring their friends, is a worthy goal. Pastors may be weighed down with the heaviness of ministry challenges, and reasonably so. But along with these challenges comes the danger of letting that heaviness infect the home, creating a cloud of seriousness that sucks the life out of a family. Don't let that happen! While ministry is serious business, it should also be a source of great joy. Give your children the blessing of a home that rejoices in the Lord always and does so by having fun. When kids can have fun with their dad, who is a pastor, they are much less likely to resent him and his "work." They will also gladly bring their friends over, creating many opportunities for hospitality and evangelism.

At appropriate times and in appropriate ways, push your children out of the nest and let them develop their own wings

One day, your children will be gone from your home. It will be just them and the Lord. Your goal for that time is that when it comes, you will have led them in such a way that they will be just fine. Many pastors' kids end up finding their identity in being part of the pastor's family, and that's not wholly a bad thing. But the time must come when they should leave the house and learn to follow Christ "on their own." You can help them do this by encouraging independence and wise decision-making, and eventually by nudging them to step out on their own.

> *Woe to the man who grows a congregation but forfeits his own children.*

Learn to regularly use seven magical words in English whenever they are needed: "I am sorry. Will you forgive me?"

We are not perfect, and our children know it. Why lie about it and lose their respect? When you blow it, admit it and ask for forgiveness. This is a sure way to raise the respect factor. As a pastor, you may feel the need to "have it all together," but your kids will know you do not. One way to model to your children your own need for the gospel you preach is by practicing regular confession and repentance before their eyes.

Pray for their salvation, and continually talk to them about Jesus and the things of God

Regularly speak the gospel to them. I had the joy of leading all four of my sons to Christ. Words cannot describe what a blessing that was. Woe to the man who grows a congregation but forfeits his own children.

I have noticed through the years that some sad and unhappy families occasionally show up at seminary. God has called dad, the family must go, and that is the end of the discussion. (Actually, the discussion never began.) To even raise a question would be a clear evidence of sin and rebellion against the will of God. So, off they go—confused, hurt, and more. In my judgment, this is not godly leadership from the man of God.

As the God-designated leader of your home, you are to lead, not drive. Surely if the Lord has called you to ministry service in the church, your family will make sacrifices, but that does not make you a dictator. Those will be their sacrifices, not yours to make for them. Furthermore, there is great wisdom for every husband and father in Proverbs 12:15, "Whoever listens to counsel is wise" (HCSB), and in Proverbs 11:14, "With many counselors there is deliverance" (HCSB). As a husband, seek your wife's counsel, her perspective. Make "we" decisions in your marriage and family. Big decisions, like moving from one ministry assignment to another, should not be made autocratically. If God is leading you to a new assignment, your wife and children need to know and believe that, too. Pray together and individually. Be united on one thing: that you will discern and obey *together* the will of God.

Don't be like too many Christian men who misunderstand the Bible, believing that leading means barking out orders and giving commands. The "my way or the highway" mentality is not only un-Christlike, it is sinful, hurtful, and ineffective. To lead you must set an example worth following. To lead as a man or pastor, you need to follow the example of Jesus (1 Cor. 11:1) as a shepherd and servant.

Pastor as Preacher

— *Jason K. Allen* —

Martyn Lloyd-Jones, the longtime pastor of Westminster Chapel in London, England, described preaching as "the highest and the greatest and the most glorious calling to which anyone can ever be called."[1] I share Lloyd-Jones's lofty assessment of preaching. The call to preach is a sacred one, and the task of preaching should be undertaken with clarity, conviction, and passion.

As this book makes clear, the modern pastor wears many hats. Yet, within the context of the local church, I believe preaching is the pastor's preeminent responsibility. Preaching is his indispensable task, his paramount duty, and his most consequential and urgent job assignment. For the pastor, preaching is priority number one.

What is more, it is not just that the pastor must preach, but that he must preach the Word. This is best accomplished through biblical exposition, which is the type of preaching we shall consider and expound upon in this essay. But first, why preaching, and why expository preaching at that?

Why Preaching?

The determination to preach the Word is first a theological commitment. We preach the Word because the Word is true, authoritative, and life-giving. Scripture is replete with this self-attestation. For instance, consider 1 Peter 1:23–25 (NASB):

> For you have been born again not of seed which is perishable but imperishable, that is, through the living and enduring word of God. For,
>
> > "All flesh is like grass,
> > And all its glory like the flower of grass.
> > The grass withers,
> > And the flower falls off,
> > But the word of the Lord endures forever."
>
> And this is the word which was preached to you.

Similarly, James testifies, "In the exercise of His will He brought us forth by the word of truth, so that we would be a kind of first fruits among His creatures" (1:18 NASB).

These passages teach us that the Lord works sovereignly in the heart of the hearer by His Spirit and through His Word. Believing this Word-Spirit dynamic is a theological commitment and thus pushes one toward biblical exposition. As Lloyd-Jones observed:

> The ultimate justification for asserting the primacy of preaching is theological. In other words, I would argue that the whole message of the Bible asserts this and drives us to this conclusion. I mean that the moment you consider man's real need, and

also the nature of salvation announced and proclaimed in the Scriptures, you are driven to the conclusion that the primary task of the church is to preach and proclaim this, to show man's real need, and to show the only remedy, the only cure for it.[2]

Lloyd-Jones is right, and that is why preaching is a consistent theme throughout Scripture and a consistent practice throughout Protestant Christianity.

A consistent theme throughout Scripture

God sent forth the prophets of old to preach. The Gospels tell us "John the Baptist appeared in the wilderness preaching a baptism of repentance" (Mark 1:4 NASB). Jesus, too, came "preaching the gospel of God" (Mark 1:14 NASB).

At Pentecost, in Acts 2, the church was birthed through Peter's preaching. Throughout the book of Acts, the apostles' preaching upended the world and fertilized the church. The office of deacon was formed to facilitate prayer and the ministry of the Word. Paul customarily went to the synagogue and reasoned from the Scriptures.

In 1 Timothy 3:2, the elder must be "able to teach." In 1 Timothy 4:13, Paul tells Timothy, "Until I come, give attention to the public reading of Scripture, to exhortation and teaching" (NASB). And,

Pastor search committees were once called "pulpit committees." A call to the ministry was a call to preach, and the pastor was often called simply "the preacher."

of course, Paul's final charge to Timothy is to "preach the word" (2 Tim. 4:2).

Most persuasively, Paul's airtight logic in Romans 10 reminds us how high the stakes truly are—it is through preaching the lost are saved. The apostle writes:

> For "whoever will call on the name of the Lord will be saved."
>
> How then will they call on Him in whom they have not believed? How will they believe in Him whom they have not heard? And how will they hear without a preacher? How will they preach unless they are sent? Just as it is written, "How beautiful are the feet of those who bring good news of good things!" (Rom. 10:13–15 NASB)

A consistent theme throughout Protestantism

The structures, functions, and history of the church—especially post-Reformation—reinforce preaching's centrality. The men who have most mightily advanced the church and shaken the world have done so through the pulpit.

As Protestants, our churches remind us of this reality as well. Our architecture places the pulpit front and center in our houses of worship. Our liturgy features preaching as the climactic point in our order of worship. Our jargon even reinforces the centrality of preaching (or at least it used to). Pastor search committees were once called "pulpit committees." A call to the ministry was a call to preach, and the pastor was often called simply "the preacher."

But if preaching is priority number one, what do we mean by preaching? How should we preach? How might we strengthen our preaching ministries?

What Is Preaching?

In *He Is Not Silent*, Albert Mohler writes, "According to the Bible, exposition is preaching. And preaching is exposition."[3] I share his assessment, and yet I must acknowledge that a consensus definition for expository preaching proves stubbornly elusive. Consequently, and regrettably, in recent years the phrase "expository preaching" has become quite elastic. Much preaching gets crammed under that heading but bears little resemblance to what more classical practitioners of biblical exposition do.

To focus our thoughts, let me suggest, minimally, four essential marks of biblical exposition:

1. The necessity of accurately interpreting the text
2. The necessity of the central point of the sermon and the sermon's main points to be derived from the text
3. The necessity of the sermon's application to come from the text and for the text to be brought to bear on the congregation
4. Fourth, and more tenuously, the priority of *lectio continua*, or sequential, verse-by-verse exposition

For example, consider how three leading homileticians define expository preaching, and listen for these common themes. Alistair Begg defines it as "unfolding the text of Scripture in such a way that makes contact with the listener's world while exalting Christ and confronting them with the need for action."[4]

Haddon Robinson's definition has been standard issue in seminary classrooms for several decades. He defines biblical exposition as "the communication of a biblical concept, derived from and transmitted through a historical, grammatical, and literary study of a passage in its context, which the Holy Spirit first applies to the personality and experience of the preacher, then through him to the hearers."[5]

Bryan Chapell argues expository preaching has occurred when

> the main idea of [the] sermon (the topic), the divisions of that idea (the main points), and the development of those divisions (the subpoints) all come from truths the text itself contains. No significant portion of the text is ignored. In other words, expositors willingly stay within the boundaries of a text (and its relevant context) and do not leave until they have surveyed its entirety with their listeners.[6]

For our purposes, we might simply define biblical exposition as *accurately interpreting and explaining the text of Scripture and bringing it to bear on the lives of the hearers*. While expository preaching can be much more than this, it cannot be anything less.

Even this minimalistic definition of expository preaching necessitates that the sermon's application be subordinate to the sermon's text. The preacher does not preach from the text or on the text, he preaches *the text*—thus limiting the sermon's application to the point of the passage preached.

While a stand-alone sermon can be an expository one, if that particular passage is handled in the aforementioned way, sequential, verse-by-verse exposition is preferred. After all, the practical wager of *lectio continua* (sequential exposition) is that over time the accrued week-to-week benefits offset the weekly adaptability and flexibility offered by topical preaching.

Now that we have defined the why and what of preaching, let's consider what it means to be a faithful preacher.

What Is a Faithful Preacher?

While I acknowledge that whole books can be written to address this question alone, let me offer at least six marks of a faithful preacher.

A faithful preacher knows his audience

In order to be a faithful preacher, you must first know your audience. Different groups in different settings often require sermons that are different in style and depth. Thus, every sermon should be a customized sermon, crafted specifically for the recipients.

When I prepare sermons, I think through exactly who will be in the audience. I bombard myself with questions like the following:

- How will this point strike the 80-year-old widow who lost her husband last year?
- Will people be able to grasp this biblical concept as presented, or do I need to simplify my explanation?
- What does this truth have to say to the young couple who is struggling with their marriage?
- How might this concept be expressed in a way that is encouraging to the middle-aged woman recently diagnosed with cancer?

Every sermon is delivered in a context, situated in a cultural moment with space and time realities. Preaching is not a sterile or clinical act. That is why seminary preaching labs can only accomplish so much. They are artificial, synthetic settings.

We do not preach to impersonal groups, but to individuals with circumstantial concerns, distractions, questions, needs, and urgencies. The aim of the sermon is to speak the Word specifically to them, the gathered crowd. The Word is powerful enough to be preached anywhere and anytime with effect, but our full confidence in the preached Word should not minimize the need for the sermon to be tailored for the specific moment.

The goal of the sermon is to change those who hear it. As York and Decker note, "Sermons are not about just imparting information. They should be custom-built to change lives. We don't want to fill their heads; we want the proclamation of the Word to grip their souls and motivate them to conform to the will of God."[7]

In fact, apostolic preaching was strikingly contextual. Peter and Paul heralded the foundational truths of the Christian faith, like the death, burial, and resurrection of Christ and salvation by repentance and faith. Yet as they preached, they engaged their audiences. This follows suit with the New Testament Epistles, each of which were written to address specific concerns facing believers, doctrinal or otherwise.

A faithful preacher takes the time to interpret the text

Faithful preaching requires being familiar, broadly speaking, with the text or book you are preaching. This familiarization takes place at both the macro and the micro level. At the macro level, it means having the big picture of the text clear in the mind. One way to accomplish this is by keeping track of context. For example, when preaching through a book of the Bible, I read through it at least twice in a row. Additionally, I pursue commentaries and other resources early on to help familiarize myself with the contours of the book.

Obviously, as my sermon preparation progresses, I will move from broad familiarization to a more technical analysis of the passage. Nonetheless, at this point, I am already trying to familiarize myself with the main idea of the text. Even though I may not reach a conclusion until after I have done more exegetical work, I am already asking myself, *What is the author saying in this passage?*

One way to grasp the "big idea" of a text is to try to write it out in one sentence. I personally have found that the earlier in the process that I wrestle with and produce the central proposition of the text, the sooner the other components of the sermon will crystallize in my mind.

Faithful preaching is built upon faithful interpretation. Few things frighten me more than the possibility of misunderstanding or misrepresenting God's Word. While no preacher bats 1000, if I err in interpreting the text, it should be because of the complexity of the passage, not the paucity of my study. In fact, over the years there have been a few times when I've aborted a sermon last minute because I was not confident I rightly understood the meaning of the text. On those occasions, I was forced to preach an old sermon, but I would rather preach a repeat sermon than an errant one.

As has been said, a fog in the pulpit is a mist in the pew. If you cannot clearly state the meaning of the passage, the main points of the sermon, and how the latter are derived from the former, you still have work to do. Moreover, twenty-dollar words and lofty concepts impress no one. Yet we do not have to forfeit the Christian dictionary in the process, either. Explain words like *redemption*, *propitiation*, and *justification*, but jettison words and concepts that are needlessly confusing. Great preaching simplifies the complicated; it doesn't complicate the simple.

A faithful preacher structures his sermon around the theme of the text

Faithful preaching involves structuring your sermon around the structure of the text. Not all sermons will, or should, sound the same. The surest way you can confirm that your sermon structure is textually oriented is to preach expositionally. As you do, the theme and contours of the text will become apparent, and as a result, they will drive your outline.

A pertinent question along these lines is, "Do my illustrations amplify or detract from the text?" To illustrate is to play with fire. When contained and rightly calibrated, good illustrations can add light and heat to the sermon. When uncontained and overtorqued, they can consume and destroy the sermon. Balance here is key. Ponder this question carefully: "Will this illustration illuminate or overshadow what the text says?" Keep your illustrations tied closely to your structure, and you will likely avoid error. And whatever you do, never illustrate an illustration.

> *Preaching is more than a data dump. . . . We are to present the text with force—probing, pushing, and prodding our listeners.*

A faithful preacher is courageous

Preaching is God's appointed means to strengthen the church and convert the lost. In every generation, the church needs pastors who preach with courage and fervency, who view preaching as the center of their ministry. Courage is essential to being a faithful preacher.

I love the way 2 Timothy 4:2 encapsulates this courage. Recall the backdrop of the book. Timothy, a young man who is probably in his early 30s, is clearly discouraged and second-guessing himself, so Paul is writing in a prophetic, apostolic way and in essence saying, "Buck up." He is challenging him. He is exhorting him to do this. He is reminding him of his rootedness in Scripture, his call to stand on Scripture and preach it.

Then he moves into how to preach the Scripture and bring it to bear on his hearers: "Preach the word; be ready in season and out of season; reprove, rebuke, and exhort, with complete patience and teaching" (4:2).

Notice the word *preach*. To preach means "to herald or to proclaim, to speak intensely." It comes with a force that presupposes courage. It is not so much the modulation of one's voice but the force of the words, weighted with conviction because you are proclaiming God's very Word.

Preaching is more than a data dump. The central liability of many expositional sermons is just that. It is a rambling commentary that drops data on people, and preachers cannot figure out why people are getting bored. We are to present the text with force—probing, pushing, and prodding our listeners. It is more than transmitting what you read in the commentaries to your people that week. It is to take it and apply it with a "Thus sayeth the Lord" charge.

A number of years ago, I took my wife to Chicago for our anniversary. We spent the weekend there. We love Chicago, and when we have the chance to go for a couple days, we take it. While there, we signed up to take an architectural boat tour. It was fascinating.

The guide on the microphone tells you that you are going by the Merchandise Mart building, and how it was built in the 20s and

30s. Before the Pentagon, it was the largest building in the United States. The Kennedy family owned it for years, and they sold it and made $450 million. You then pass by the Sears Tower (now the Willis Tower), and on and on. You go through the city by water, and the guide tells you about the river and the skyline and every building and its architectural rendering and style, so that by the end you are left with hordes of data about the city.

Often I hear preaching like that. It is merely cruising through the passage, giving a little historical background, a contextual statement here, a little word study there, and an "exegetical fallacy" there (to borrow a D. A. Carson phrase). You leave saying, "Hmm, that was enlightening."

Do you see the problem? Preaching should never be less than a Bible study, but it should always be more than a Bible study. It is more than a boat tour or an architectural assessment of the passage. We are doing more than revealing artifacts; we are bringing the passage to bear. All of this should be done with conviction and courage.

Mark your life and set yourself to preach with courage.

A faithful preacher connects the text to the gospel

As gospel preachers, every sermon should contain the gospel. Usually this happens quite naturally and organically within the text itself. You don't have to be an archaeologist to find Christ in the text; you just have to open your eyes.

Paul's ambition to preach Christ and Him crucified (1 Cor. 2:2) should be ours as well, and we can best accomplish this by not just preaching "gospel" messages or tacking on the gospel at the end of our sermon. To rightly interpret any text is to draw lines from that text to the broader, biblical metanarrative of Christ and Him crucified. Therefore, to preach an Old Testament narrative or a New

Testament epistle should not be a detour from the gospel. Rather, it should be an inroad to it. Every sermon based on Scripture is a sermon in which Christ can be rightfully and prominently featured.

A faithful preacher grows in his craft

Biblical exposition isn't easy. It takes time to interpret the passage in its context, build an exegetical outline, and fashion it all together in homiletical form. And then you have to deliver it—a craft in and of itself.

Year after year, the rigor of preparing sermons has deepened my scriptural knowledge. The thousands of hours wrestling with texts have been incalculably sanctifying. Moreover, preaching verse by verse through books in the Bible forces me to confront difficult doctrines, grapple with knotty texts, and apply the full complement of Scripture to my own life. Plus, regularly delivering sermons has knit my heart to my community and allowed me to grow as a preacher.

All of this, and more, facilitates spiritual growth and maturation—not just for the preacher, but for his hearers. The more we develop in our craft, the more others are built up. Thus, a faithful preacher will not tire in refining his ability to divide and deliver the Word of truth.

In his famous book *On the Preparation and Delivery of Sermons*, John Broadus observed:

In the ministry of Jesus, preaching was central. Although greatly tempted to give primacy to other methods of approach to the world, he "came preaching." . . .

And for their mission after him, he gave his apostles the same strategy. . . .

The great increase and availability of books, magazines, and newspapers, the reach of the radio, the appeal of the motion picture, the instant availability of television, have seemed to many to depreciate preaching . . . but they cannot be substituted for it. . . .

It follows that preaching is always a necessity, for preaching is inextricably linked to the life of the church.[8]

And so it is. Preaching is God's appointed means to strengthen the church and save the lost. In every generation, the church needs pastors who preach with courage and fervency, who view preaching as the center of their ministry. Indeed, for the pastor, preaching is priority number one.

After all, as Broadus observed, if preaching was primary in Jesus' ministry, ought it not be primary in ours?

Pastor as Theologian

— *Owen D. Strachan* —

W here does the pastor fit in modern America? Pastors are a strange people today. They are not at home in the academy, for the academy long ago boxed theology up and removed it from the realm of higher learning. They are not home in the public square, for their brand of thinking is rigorously biblical and thus viewed as culturally inflexible. They are not at home in the world of arts and letters, for they supposedly care nothing about the intellect, aesthetics, and culture. For many people, the word *pastor* conjures up images of an uncouth, insensitive bore—a profile that popular culture has been eager to propagate in recent decades.

The demotion of the pastor in American and even Western cultural life is likely the most significant intellectual trend of the last five hundred years. Pastors have gone, in broad terms, from being the key thinkers and leaders of the community to unnoticed and unwanted outsiders. In such dire circumstances, the pastorate

You could be forgiven for thinking that the pastorate finds its horsepower in business practices, arena-rock musical extravaganzas, expertly curated programs, radical acts, political involvement, mercy ministries, cultural engagement, funny stories, hipster affectations, folksy, down-to-earth demeanors, and a hundred other areas.

as a vocation has lost much of its essential identity and much of its inherent glory.[1]

Pastors today feel impotent. They sense no great weight in their words. They feel as if they must add something to the Bible if they are to draw a crowd and gain a hearing. So pastors become chameleons, practitioners of diverse and sometimes non-intersecting skill sets. These days you could be forgiven for thinking that the pastorate finds its horsepower in business practices, arena-rock musical extravaganzas, expertly curated programs, radical acts, political involvement, mercy ministries, cultural engagement, funny stories, hipster affectations, folksy, down-to-earth demeanors, and a hundred other areas.

In our time, the biblical pastor feels ill at ease in his skin, in his calling. He loves the Word, but he has been told that it has lost its power. Perhaps secularism is too strong. Perhaps worldly lusts have overcome the appeal of the Scriptures. Perhaps our attention spans have changed, and people simply cannot sit still to listen to forty-minute sermons filled with doctrine and exegesis.

It is understandable that the pastor feels discouraged today, but there is great encouragement before us as well: we have not lost our birthright. The ministry may flare with life once more. The pastor may rise from the ashes. He may do so by recognizing this one truth: there is only one source of true pastoral power. This source is the gospel of grace, the message of Christ's crucifixion and resurrection, which brings salvation to Adam's fallen race (Rom. 5:12–21). So it always has been. The good news *for us* is that the good news works *in us* and *through us*. It is that simple. This—not platforms, growth charts, top-40 church rankings, or any other metric or means—is our hope.

In 2 Timothy, the aged apostle Paul reminds his disciple Timothy of this reality. For Paul, the pastor is a theologian—a theologian serving Christ's church—who is given the very oracles of God to save sinners and build up the faithful. In what follows, we will briefly study 2 Timothy 1:5–14, finding here a threefold elaboration of what it means for the pastor to be a theologian. First, in verses 5–7 we discover the need for spiritual ambition, learning the *attitude* of the pastor-theologian. Second, in verses 8–12 we learn how the gospel powers the pastorate, unearthing the *confidence* of the pastor-theologian. Third, in verses 13–14 we note that the pastorate summons us to play theological offense and defense, revealing the essential *work* of the pastor-theologian.

The Attitude of the Pastor-Theologian: Holy Ambition (vv. 5–7)

I am reminded of your sincere faith, a faith that dwelt first in your grandmother Lois and your mother Eunice and now, I am sure, dwells in you as well. For this reason I remind you to fan into flame the gift of God, which is in you through the laying on of my hands, for God gave us a spirit not of fear but of power and love and self-control.

Second Timothy is a letter that unfolds the identity of the pastor. In framing who the pastor is, Paul first gives his charge a shot in the arm. He calls attention to the faith of Timothy's mother and grandmother and challenges him to be fearless in God. He reminds Timothy of his gifting, a gifting conferred and confirmed by an apostle of the living Christ. John Stott suggests that this gifting is "both the office of pastor and the spiritual equipment needed to fulfill it."[2] Stott's take shows us the weight of this gift. The pastoral deposit, given by God, is not a passive one. To the contrary, it must be "fan[ned] into flame" (v. 6), which means that the instinct in young men to find a pulpit is fundamentally a good one.

The pastorate is an office that comes with high expectations. This is a biblical model: to train men by challenging them to meet a standard higher than they think they can reach. The scriptural perspective on pastoral preparation is less like that of a sports league that grants everyone a trophy and more like a Navy SEAL program. Granted, there are no all-night-sitting-in-water drills or push-up requirements that leave your arms like jelly, but the point stands: God fundamentally challenges the future shepherds of His church. Like the young athlete discovering his abilities in the heat of the moment, we want young men to want the ball, to hunger to enter a pulpit and proclaim the mysteries of God. The God who is a consuming fire wants preachers who burn with passion for Him.[3]

The young preacher will no doubt feel such passion in his veins. But we are complex creatures, and undoubtedly "fear"

(v. 7) and shame will conspire to quiet the young preacher—even Timothy faced these demons. As noted earlier, we find ourselves in a day when many pastors feel fear. They feel defeated. Culture has become incredibly secularized, and evangelical pastors are not the honored guests at the cultural dinner party. Pastors represent an older, hierarchical era when people believed in authority. But confidence in authority—at least religious authority—is at an all-time low in America. When confidence in the authority of God dips, the glory of the pastorate dims.

As a result, ministry is seen as just one of many "helping professions." This is precisely what happened in the early twentieth century. Interest in theology waned, business culture boomed, and pastors were forced to adapt to an urbanizing America to draw a crowd. This shift from theological ministry to "practical ministry" had huge effects among Baptists, including (for some) a loss of confidence in the Word of God. Thankfully, the centrality of Scripture in the life of the local church was revived in the "Conservative Resurgence" of the 1980s. But we have work to do in our time. We have recovered the doctrine of inerrancy; now we must recover a doctrine of the pastorate. The Conservative Resurgence returned to the *formal authority* of Scripture; now we must believe once more in the *functional authority* of Scripture. The solution to the fear and shame we may naturally feel is found in remembering what God has given us.[4]

Thankfully, God has not left us alone. He has given us a system of mentoring such that men like Paul lift the flagging hands of young men like Timothy. Our need to challenge young men to assume a higher call in no way removes our need to love and strengthen our disciples when they struggle. We see the apostle carrying out just this kind of work with Timothy. He reminds his charge that God has given us a spirit of "power and love and self-control" (v. 7). It is this kind of mentality that Scripture births in us—not a play-it-safe mentality, but a disciplined, risk-it-all approach. The work of Christ in us creates strong character. It makes us strong over sin, loving instead of angry, and disciplined instead of dissolute. The character that God forges internally is the same character that can take the heat externally. The pastor-theologian has spiritual ambition and strong, godly character. The mark of a pastor, even a young one, is that of godliness, including a willingness to put everything on the line in order to give Christ the glory He deserves.

The Confidence of the Pastor-Theologian: Grounded in the Gospel (vv. 8–12)

Therefore do not be ashamed of the testimony about our Lord, nor of me his prisoner, but share in suffering for the gospel by the power of God, who saved us and called us to a holy calling, not because of our works but because of his own purpose and grace, which he gave us in Christ Jesus before the ages began, and which now has been manifested through the appearing of our Savior Christ Jesus, who abolished death and brought life and immortality to light through the gospel, for which I was appointed a preacher and apostle and teacher, which is why I suffer as I do. But I am not ashamed, for I know whom I have believed, and I am convinced that he is able to guard until that day what has been entrusted to me.

Paul the apostle doesn't speak like a morning talk-show host, all hyperbole and flattery. He speaks like a military general. He has been through the fire. In calling Timothy to theocentric pastoral ministry, he is calling the young man to walk through the fire, too. He knows the stakes of this vocation are high—impossibly high. So he counsels his disciple, "Do not be ashamed" (v. 8). We can infer here that Timothy was likely tempted to feel shame at a personal level. But we also know this: every pastor will face the same temptation, and every Christian will as well.

The call to ministry is a call to kill shame. We all are tempted to move away from those who have their doorposts painted red. The body of Christ stands out in a fallen world just as the Israelites stood out in Egypt. In a world of towering intellects and neo-atheist voices, the gospel can seem like a small, silly message. This has always been true in this realm. In an ancient context, being imprisoned would indicate the defeat and foolishness of the prisoner's worldview, but note how Paul describes himself. He is "his [God's] prisoner" (v. 8), God's servant appointed to suffer in jail. But his suffering is not his own. Timothy is called to "share in suffering" (v. 8). This suffering is not because of idiocy, poor tactics, sin, or weak brand management. It is because of the gospel.

There is a great contrast in play here in verses 8–9. On the one hand, the young pastor can hold a chastened, fearful take on gospel ministry. On the other, he can see the Christian life, and by extension the ministry, as a "holy calling" (v. 9). There is glorious theology loaded into this conception. The Father "gave" this calling to us "in Christ Jesus before the ages began" (v. 9). Divine sovereignty underwrites all of Timothy's ministry. Paul is saying this: God has planned this call. It is his. Timothy simply has to walk in it.

The pastorate Timothy assumes is grounded in the holy gospel. This is what Paul communicates in verses 9–12. God's "purpose and grace" (v. 9) have been manifested through Christ.

Christ has accomplished His work, as Paul emphasizes by using several hard verbs. Jesus "abolished" death and "brought life and immortality to light" (v. 10). The work of the pastor is an extension of this ministry: in union with Christ, the pastor announces the abolition of death and the dawning of life. Gordon Fee says it this way: "Our last enemy, death, has already received its mortal wound."[5] Death has died through the death of Jesus Christ. Jesus' sacrificial atonement has cleansed us of our sin; His vicarious resurrection has given us power over the grave. He has given us His righteousness and taken our sin; we have received His righteousness and given Him our sin. By the repentance and faith granted us, we are saved, forgiven, adopted, regenerated, and justified. This is the message we preach; this is the core of our life, the substance of our hope, and the heart of our identity.[6]

This is the freedom in which we live. This is the power of the gospel that the pastor holds in his hand. According to John Calvin, because the pastor ministers the authoritative Word and the exclusive gospel, he has tremendous spiritual influence:

> Here, then, is the sovereign power with which the pastors of the church, by whatever name they be called, ought to be endowed. That is that they may dare boldly to do all things by God's Word; may compel all worldly power, glory, wisdom, and exaltation to yield to and obey his majesty; supported by his power, may command all from the highest even to the last; may build up Christ's household and cast down Satan's; may feed the sheep and drive away the wolves; may instruct and exhort the teachable; may accuse, rebuke, and subdue the rebellious and stubborn; may bind and loose; finally, if need be, may launch thunderbolts and lightnings; but do all things in God's Word.[7]

We note the effect of the gospel, how powerful it is. But we note as well where this forcefulness is: it is in the Word. It stems from the authority of God. It flows from the inspiration of the Spirit. It proceeds from the preaching of Scripture. Hear Spurgeon on this point:

> No system can be a form of sound words unless it is perfectly scriptural. We receive no doctrines as the doctrines of men; whatever authority come to us which is not the authority of the Holy Spirit, and inspired by God, is no authority at all to us. . . . If our opponent cannot quote text or verse for anything he advances, we hold no argument with him. Scripture is the only weapon we can acknowledge.[8]

All the horsepower of ministry comes from the Word of God. Paul was appointed to a Word-centered, gospel-celebrating ministry. Note that the word *appointed* wasn't only an internal compulsion. The predominant factor in entering the ministry is absolute, divine sovereignty. Thomas Oden says it well. As opposed to one who sidles up to the ministry, the preacher "is more like one who has been awakened from sleep and summoned."[9] How true this was of Paul. Before his spectacular conversion, Paul was trying to destroy preachers, not develop them. But God had another plan. The summons to ministry for the pastor may, of course, not be as radical as Paul's was, but it owes no less to divine sovereignty than Paul's. It is not only the creation of the cosmos that God oversees in His power and wisdom. The Lord superintends and guides every facet of life, including the call to gospel work.[10] What a comfort this is for those seeking to discern whether God would have them serve Him in the ministry.

It was for nothing else but the message of Christ that Paul took his apostolic place. Paul says it was the gospel "for which [he] was appointed a preacher and apostle and teacher" (v. 11). Surely this was a call unique to Paul, but note what he was: alongside being an apostle, he was a preacher and teacher. His roles proceed not from a vague interest in spiritual things, nor from a willingness to dally in meditation and mindfulness, but from the gospel. For Paul, there is no pastorate without the gospel.

So it is with us. The role of apostle was unique to the era of Christ. There is no system in place given in the New Testament for the selection of the next generation of apostles. There is, however, a setup clear as a bell at midday for the appointing of elders and deacons (see 1 Timothy 3, for example). Though Timothy is not an apostle (he would have been a prime candidate to be one, of course, given his close connection to Paul), he is assuredly a preacher and teacher. These roles continue past the first century. Though we modern men do not serve as Paul did in an apostolic role, we have the privilege of serving as preachers and teachers of the flock of God. What an impossible gift this is; what a joy to proclaim Christ in any setting and status—great or small, paid or unpaid, known by many or as anonymous as a blade of grass in a rolling field.

The ministry is glorious, to be sure. But in a sin-cursed world, Christic proclamation is not going to win you friends in high places. In verse 12, Paul returns to the dual theme of suffering and shame he introduced in verse 8: "[Being a preacher, apostle, and teacher] is why I suffer as I do. But I am not ashamed, for I know whom I have believed." The proclamation of the gospel *should* produce exultation, but it doesn't. It means suffering like Paul did. To be a pastor-theologian doesn't mean leaving the people, sitting in an ivory tower with Restoration Hardware furniture, sipping your craft coffee, and winning plaudits from secularists. It means suffering. It means people hate you. It means they may want to kill you.

We do not offer people a theology of glory by which they make their lives materially awesome. We offer people a theology of the cross, as Martin Luther so well said, by which their souls are saved, if necessary by fire.[11] The gospel we preach might well make their lives easier as they embrace it. But note this: it might also make their lives harder. We have followed Jesus "outside the camp." We live with him now (Heb. 13:13).

The pastor is a theologian, but not a theologian of upward mobility. The pastor is a theologian of the cross. We cannot ever forget this: we have left the path of cultural acclaim and top-100 churches and societal approval. It is not that we seek to be as hated as possible for no good reason. We strive to lead a quiet life and to be at peace with all (1 Tim. 2:2). But the situation we face is that proclamation of Christ will lead us directly into conflict with spiritual forces. So it is that most of the apostles were martyred. So it was that our Lord Himself was crucified. In a time of great economic prosperity, when many people simply want to live and let live, the Christian has a higher call, and the Christian preacher is the one who announces it.

If you know that your soul is secure, you will walk into a lion's den, a fiery furnace, a Roman colosseum, or an American courtroom.

Paul knew this. But as he writes to his disciple, Paul has great hope. Come what may, Paul knows his God (v. 12). The fact that God is totally in control, "able to guard" the entrusted gospel until "that day," fills him with hope and scrubs him of shame. It was not up to Paul to perform brand management for the kingdom of Christ. His God was fully capable of doing that Himself. He was not only positively disposed to the gospel message, but He had full power to guard and protect it, and so He has. What a comfort this was for the apostle. What a comfort it is for pastors today. The doctrine of divine sovereignty is *the* foundation for all encouragement in the Christian life. If you know that God rules over history and has a day ("that day" in v. 12) when His Son will return and gather His people to Himself, you will do anything for Him. If you know that your soul is secure, you will walk into a lion's den, a fiery furnace, a Roman colosseum, or an American courtroom.

The pastor-theologian is grounded in the gospel, and it is in the end the gospel—or rather, the God of the gospel—who is his confidence.

The Work of the Pastor-Theologian: Theological Offense and Defense (vv. 13–14)

Follow the pattern of the sound words that you have heard from me, in the faith and love that are in Christ Jesus. By the Holy Spirit who dwells within us, guard the good deposit entrusted to you.

There are two tasks allotted to Timothy, and to every pastor, in our final section. First, Timothy needs to follow Paul. But this following, like every concept in this passage, is theological—through "the pattern of the sound words" (v. 13), which refers to the teaching of the Spirit given to Paul. The Greek word here for "sound" is used of people healed in the gospel by Jesus. Marvel at the power of the Word and the gospel: it has the power to heal to the uttermost. This is why Timothy must follow it.

All that Paul has been taught he hands down to Timothy, who is charged to hand it down to the church. This is a deeply personal teaching, which is what pastoral ministry entails. It is not green-screen teaching. It is flesh-and-blood teaching. It is teaching that is married with life. So it is with every pastor—the ideal for our ministries is not that of a disembodied hologram glimpsed on a screen, but that of personal holiness exercised to and for people who know us.[12]

Such potent work will naturally receive profound response from the devil. There are two major avenues of attack planned by Satan on every pastor. The first is a softening of doctrine; the second is a softening of morality. In truth, one often activates the other. We watch our life and doctrine closely (1 Tim. 4:16). The two go hand in hand. There was no slippage morally for Paul. He called Timothy to truth—sound doctrine—and to holy living.

Through union with Jesus, we have His "purpose and grace" (v. 9) and we have "faith and love" (v. 13). This is anything but a self-sufficient ministry. This is the opposite of a "bootstrap" mentality. All the good that is in you as a Christian and a pastor is from God. The pastor promotes the "in-Christ" life. He plays offense against the devil. He doesn't leave his people to get attacked. He has hope and confidence as he ministers. His hope is in Christ. His confidence is in the gospel. He does not promote himself; he points his people to God. All this is inescapably *theological* work.

If the first task of a pastor's theological ministry concerns playing offense—that is, promoting the truth—the second concerns playing defense—guarding the truth. By the Spirit's power, Paul exhorts Timothy to "guard the good deposit" (v. 14). Matthew

Henry rightly notes that the deposit "is committed to Christians in general, but ministers in particular."[13] Note the qualification for defending the truth of Christ: the Spirit's indwelling power. It is not a degree; it is not a writing ministry; it is not a fancy pedigree that equips you to ward off the roaring lion who would devour you and your people. It is the Holy Spirit. This work is focused on preserving the gospel of grace. If Satan can undermine our confidence in the gospel, which is the power of God unto salvation, he can undermine our confidence in anything of God.

We need to recognize just how powerful the Spirit's gifting is. The Spirit is the activator and the guarantor of the pastor-theologian. The Spirit equips us to be the theologian-in-residence of our congregation. The Spirit enables us to be the ethicist of our congregation. The Spirit empowers us to be the worldview shaper of our congregation.[14]

For youth drawn to a fake vision of the sexual revolution, we offer freedom. For fathers enticed by a boyish fantasy culture of endless sex and sports, we offer holiness. For women encouraged to think of their worth in worldly terms, we offer truth. For workers drawn to despise their work, we offer the biblical doctrine of vocation. For Christians told not to trust the doctrine of Scripture, we offer theology. For believers told that the atonement of Christ is "divine child abuse," we offer the theology of substitutionary sacrifice, a scandal to the world but the living hope of the church. For people told that their works earn merit in the process of justification, we offer the gospel. For those suffering from the weight of past abuse and suffering, we offer theistic hope.[15]

The help we offer in these and every circumstance is the gospel of the Word. We regularly hear today that the Word isn't enough. Jesus isn't enough. The Scripture that declares the gospel isn't trustworthy anymore. The "new theology" of the Enlightenment supposedly destroyed belief in miracles; then the "new theology" of the late nineteenth century rendered scriptural inspiration obsolete. Then the "modernist theology" psychologized the faith and made truth claims out of vogue. Then the "death of God" theology announced, well, the death of God.

You could sum up these trends like this: the new theology is old news. But here's what is enduring and relevant for us: Jesus. He is enough. He is never out of style. He is never outmoded. There is no greater Savior. There is no higher truth than Him. So, promote the truth. Defend the truth. Be who you are: a pastor and a theologian. You never show your identity more then when you promote the "in-Christ" life and guard the good deposit from every revision and edit.

Applications

With our study of 2 Timothy 1 complete, I offer now just four short points of application for pastors eager to follow the charge to be faithful, zealous theologians.

Every pastor-theologian unfolds the glory of Christ—a glory hidden from the world that will soon be revealed

This is primarily what we mean by saying the pastor is a theologian: the pastor preaches Christ. As we have seen, the world cannot comprehend the glory of the resurrected Messiah. This is a hidden glory, and we preach a hidden kingdom. But our preaching is not benign to lost people. The whole world lies under the spell of Satan, and so we must suffer in preaching. The call that is above every call is nonetheless a call to suffer and die.

We think here of what faithfulness to Christ meant for our past heroes. For Luther, it meant the threat of death. For Calvin, it meant he could not return to his home. For many of the Anabaptists, it meant death. For Jonathan Edwards, it meant being fired. For Spurgeon, it meant being hated. For J. C. Ryle, it meant his own son disowning his regressive theology. For John Machen, it meant the loss of Princeton and an early death. We must thus ask of ourselves, "What will the scandal of Christ, and the scandalous preaching of this scandal, mean for us?"

We fear man not simply in swallowing our evangelistic witness on the airplane; we fear man when we quaver over standing alone, without our peers, on doctrinal matters. In 1889, Ryle noted this:

> A wave of colour blindness about theology appears to be passing over the land. The minds of many seem utterly incapable of discerning any difference between faith and faith, creed and creed, tenet and tenet . . . however diverse, heterogeneous, contrariant, and mutually destructive they may be. . . . You are not allowed to ask what is God's truth, but what is liberal, and generous, and kind. These people live in a kind of mist or fog. . . . They are eaten up with a morbid dread of CONTROVERSY and an ignorant dislike of PARTY SPIRIT, and they really cannot define what they mean by these phrases.[16]

Ryle's blunt, old-style speech instructs us today and upbraids our natural fear of what people think of us. How common this problem is in our time: the fear of man. Our central concern, however, is never our poll numbers, our Q rating with our congregation. It is always the truth of God, which leads to the restoration of man.

Because the pastor stands on the firm ground of sound doctrine, his position will hold. The pastor is a theologian, not a poll-taker. He does not worry about his reputation, image, or brand. Jesus is the pastor's brand. The gospel is the pastor's message. The cross is the pastor's image.

The pastor-theologian holds an office for mature men

We are not playing at ministry. We are stewarding life-and-death realities. The ministry is very hard work. This means that we pray to God for a spirit of power and love and self-control. It means we act maturely. Too often today, we locate the horsepower for ministry in less important aspects of our lives: the way we dress, the image others associate with us, the connections we have. It's normal and good to have preferences—even if you wear aggressively normal cargo shorts, a common fashion inclination of many ministers. But the pastor is suited for ministry not by the brand he presents, but by holy character and tested maturity.

Inevitably in life, there are times when the going gets tough. In such instances, we may want to shrink back. We can all understand this temptation. What pastors must remember, though, is that trials are opportunities for the experience of grace. All pastors will feel frail and weak at times, but in truth we have access to a greater strength than anything the world offers. We have the indwelling Spirit (Rom. 8:9ff). We have abiding help and power for godliness. We are thus able by the sheer grace of God to keep going.

God has worked in the pastor to make him mature, to develop self-control, and to produce a persevering spirit. There is nothing fancy about a mature man of this caliber. Yet this is what the pastorate demands: strong fiber. A willingness to endure hardship. A constant dependence on God borne of the biblical truth that God makes His pastors—indeed, all His church—strong by the Spirit's work. These traits are not what the world typically celebrates, but they are the very core of pastoral character, and they will sustain the man of God in tough seasons.

Pastor-theologians seek to grow in their grasp of God's Word

Pastors need to study to show that they are approved and can skillfully handle the Word (2 Tim. 2:15). This means a full-scale, long-term approach to pastoral theological development. We must give priority to textual exposition, but we must also develop the congregation's understanding of biblical theology. This means that we help our people to read the Scripture aright and that we offer them a richly developed understanding of the newness of the new covenant.[17] We want the church to understand that it is not under old covenant law, but is bound by the law of Christ—the law of love, for example (see John 13:34). The pastor, we remember, is the one who builds his people's theology. He does this week by week, text by text.

The pastor is a thinker. Thus, the pastor needs to be a reader. He may carve out time in his schedule for stimulating books. He may keep up on current trends, reading outlets like the *Wall Street Journal, New York Times*, and the Gospel Coalition. The pastor can build a library bit by bit, reading widely in a range of disciplines over time—some fiction, some philosophy, some biography, some leadership. The pastor can avail himself of the many strong conferences offered today, traveling a couple times per year to be fed and encouraged. The pastor should not see himself as a static figure, but as a lifelong learner and pedagogue to his people.

Every pastor ministers theology, for there is nothing else to minister

In counseling, evangelism, and discipleship, this is what we have to offer—this and nothing else. Take away Christ, and we do not exist. Take away the gospel, and this office—*poof!*—vanishes into thin air. See the magisterial words of Jonathan Edwards:

> The business of the Gospel is properly a divine business. They that are called to this work are called to a work that may properly be called Christ's work. It is a business wherein a person has, in all parts of it, to do with God. It is either to act in the name of God's people towards God, or in the name of God towards the people. It all consists in acting either to God or from God. And it is to act for God. God is more immediately the end of the work of the ministry than of any other work or employment that men are called to in this world.[18]

This is profoundly true in the local church, the laboratory of theology. But this is true for the church on a broader scale. We obey Scripture, which contains all that we need for life and godliness (2 Peter 1:3–11). We take wisdom wherever we find it, but we do not sit back and ask secular professionals to put sinners back together who have been ruined by depravity. We alone are those who steward, preach, and apply the Word and gospel. We act *for God*. We must regain this aspect of the pastor's role today, and we must make good on it in our ministry and practice.

There is nothing else the world needs but the truth of God. Doctrine—being the truth of God—is our hope. It is doctrine that saved us; it is doctrine that is guarding and growing our churches; and it is doctrine that is going to preserve us as we head into the open sea of the twenty-first century. We have no other hope. We have nothing else to stand on. We have sound biblical doctrine, and that is all we need. This is the confession and the confidence of the pastor-theologian.

In modern America, where does the pastor fit? The world may say that the pastor is a humble, fragile, insignificant figure. He is out of place in the twenty-first century. Sure, secular culture may recognize pastors who seem impressive by its standards: big salaries, big megaphones, big accomplishments. But what about pastors of churches (big or small in numerical number) who simply preach Christ, love their people, and evangelize the lost? What about pastors who do not bow the knee to the culture?

The world may ignore or deride such figures. But pastors of this type—the true type, shaped by the true man, Jesus Christ—are not forgotten by God. He sees them now. He uses them here. He has a place for them in His kingdom—set your watch by that. Very soon, He will reward them when He returns, when the whole earth becomes His footstool, and when the godly efforts of every pastor seem small—impossibly small—in light of the Greater Shepherd.

Pastor as Church Historian

— *Christian T. George* —

*Moses took the bones of Joseph with him because Joseph
had made the Israelites swear an oath. He had said,
"God will surely come to your aid, and then you must
carry my bones up with you from this place."*
EXODUS 13:19 NIV

Once upon a time, Noah looked up to see a rainbow arc across the horizon (Gen. 9:12–16). Abraham also raised his gaze as God said, "I will make your descendants as numerous as the stars in the sky" (Gen. 26:4 NIV). But now, after four centuries of bondage, the only thing above God's people was the blazing Egyptian sun. Had Yahweh forgotten His faithfulness? Was divinity suffering from dementia? Where were the promises?

Then Moses saw fire burning in a desert bush. Yahweh went

on the offensive. He sent His prophet and then His plagues. He even lit His people's path by a pillar of fire. Yet there is a subtle detail often overlooked in the Exodus account. As the Jews departed for the Promised Land, they packed the bones of Joseph. Have you ever wondered why they bothered to bring those bones? Why not use the space and energy to bring food, water, tents, and other critical supplies? Why burn the calories carrying around a bag of bones?

Because those were not just anyone's bones. Those were *Joseph's* bones. Those were the bones of their ancestor who, like them, was sold into slavery before being rescued by God (Gen. 41:41–46). Those bones of Joseph reminded God's people who they were—not Egyptians, but Jews. They did not worship the sun god, Amun-Ra; they worshiped the one true God, Yahweh. The DNA of God's promise to Abraham was still fresh in the marrow of those bones. That skeleton was just as essential as food or water because it kept alive their identity as the chosen people of God.

You and I must bring along a bag of bones as well. We must remember who we are and *whose* we are. That is why every pastor *must* be a church historian. You are responsible for steering the hearse of history, for transporting the bones of the past into the territory of tomorrow. If we forget where we came from—our history and heritage—we will not be equipped for where we are going. If we forget our past and its mistakes, our churches are bound to repeat them. The discipline of church history is one of the most important navigational tools a pastor can own. In this chapter, we will explore its definition and application by examining *what* church history is, *why* every pastor should be a church historian, and *how* you can practically implement this discipline into your life and ministry.

What Is Church History?

If Augustine of Hippo was right that "the church has gone forward on pilgrimage amid the persecution of the world and the consolation of God,"[1] then church history is simply the retelling of that pilgrimage. Church history is not the study of *our* story so much as it is the study of God's story.

And what a marvelous story it is. Church history is the story of how God raised up shepherds and scholars, pastors and missionaries, and through the power of His providence delivered them from bondage to blessing. The church is not a nomad aimlessly wandering in the wilderness. Nor is she a tourist obsessed with the entertainments of the world. The church is a *pilgrim* traveling to a city—a *Celestial* City, as John Bunyan called it in his popular allegory, *The Pilgrim's Progress*.

The concept of pilgrimage helps define and refine our understanding of the church. Every page of Scripture is threaded with this penetrating theme. Since humanity was driven out of Eden, God's people have wandered through this world looking for a "city with foundations, whose architect and builder is God" (Heb. 11:10 NIV). Pilgrim psalms comforted God's people as they traveled annually to Jerusalem. Jesus Himself went on pilgrimages to celebrate Passover. When He was twelve years old, He even lingered there to teach in the temple (Luke 2:41–52). Pilgrimage became not only a physical practice but also a spiritual theme to warn God's people and encourage them in the midst of persecution. To the churches of Asia Minor, Peter wrote, "Dearly beloved, I beseech you as strangers and *pilgrims*, abstain from fleshly lusts, which war against the soul" (1 Peter 2:11 KJV).

The history of the church links together believers of all backgrounds. Like the motley crew of pilgrims traveling to the shrine of Thomas Becket in Geoffrey Chaucer's *Canterbury Tales*, God's church contains unlikely sojourners. From the Wife of Bath to the Knight, the Priest, and the Miller, the history of the church is multicultural, complex, and colorful. For instance, what connects the North African Augustine of Hippo to his contemporary, Patrick of Ireland? Both experienced conversion later in life. Both wrote their own autobiographical *Confessions*. But Christianity in the British Isles looked nothing like Christianity in the Mediterranean. What commonality bonds their histories together?

The pastor leads his people by pushing this world into the next one, but he feeds his people by pulling the next world into this one.

The same question may be directed toward J. R. R. Tolkien's *Lord of the Rings* novels. What commonalities exist between Gandalf and Gimli, Aragorn and Samwise, or Frodo and Legolas? Though different in background, perspective, and ability, each character finds fellowship around the ring. In the same way, the history of the church is composed of pilgrims separated by geography and chronology, and yet they are forever united—not through a ring, but through a *cross*.

Church history is the story of the fellowship of the cross. Even the vilest characters—the Sméagols, if you will—have a crucial and redemptive role to play in the success of the mission.

Why Study Church History?

Church history has been called the queen of all disciplines be-cause, like an umbrella, she encompasses the rest of them. Biblical studies, homiletics, philosophy, systematics, apologetics, counsel-ing, and all other fields find their proper place beneath history's overarching reach. Because no discipline can escape the historical context in which it develops, a greater knowledge of church his-tory will amplify and edify every aspect of these disciplines. Do you want to learn more about the Bible? Study the context in which the Bible was written. The Bible itself was not only woven into the fabric of history, the Bible *is* history, for it records the dramatic story of God's interest and activity. Peter wrote, "For prophecy never had its origin in the human will, but prophets, though human, spoke from God as they were carried along by the Holy Spirit" (2 Peter 1:21 NIV). Do you want to be able to think more clearly about the doctrine of the Trinity (a word not found in the Bible, though the concept is clearly there)? Investigate the history of the second- and third-century church, and see how the church wrestled to describe the relationships among Father, Son, and Spirit. Do you want to improve your preaching? Study the ser-mons of Ambrose and Augustine, Luther and Calvin, Whitefield and Wesley, Spurgeon and Moody.

The pastor's primary role is to *lead* and *feed*. Both tasks—*exodus* ("the way out") and *exegesis* ("to lead out of")—center on journey. The pastor leads his people by pushing this world into the next one, but he feeds his people by pulling the next world into this one. He leads by moving his people from *now* to *then*, but he feeds his people by moving *then* to *now*. At the center of this journey of opposing directionalities—this pushing the present forward and pulling the future backward—is the ultimate aim of church history: retrieval for the sake of renewal and revival.

We sometimes think of church history in terms of what is behind us. But Scripture broadens our definition. Church history is the story of *all* God has done, *all* God is doing, and *all* God will do for His people. Does church history even have a beginning or ending? When did God's love for His people first commence? When will God's presence with His people conclude? From before the foundation of the world, God prepared for His people a plan of redemption and a place of fellowship, one that extends into the infinite reaches of eternity.

The task of the church historian is to proclaim this promise. The psalmist declared, "I will utter hidden things, things from of old—things we have heard and known, things our ancestors have told us. We will not hide them from their descendants; we will tell the next generation the praiseworthy deeds of the LORD, his power, and the wonders he has done" (Ps. 78:2–4 NIV). However, as we begin to recount "things from of old," three obstacles present themselves. The first is archaism.

Archaism

Archaism is when the discipline of church history collapses into the mere memorization of names, dates, and places. The temptation here is to think of history as a fossilized account of the world that bears no relevance to my church, my culture, my time, or me. How ironic! One of the greatest hindrances to the discipline of history is the one who presents it: the history teacher. How many history classes have been slept through because the professor succumbed to the temptation of archaism? We must never forget God is in the business of making dry bones live again (Ezek. 37).

As humans, you and I cannot live in the past or future. Every hour, minute, and second of our lives is experienced *in the present*. History is the study of the *right now*. Even as you read these very words, history is happening to you and around you. As

Libraries are where the dead can speak to the living.

students and teachers of God's story, we must begin to think of history not primarily as the study of the past, but instead as the study of the present, albeit other peoples' present. Church history comes to life when we realize that we are the history of tomorrow. Right now, you are part of God's ongoing mission in this world. Like a paragraph in a novel, your life connects what is behind you to what is before you. As stewards *of* the story and actors *in* the story, your contribution is just as important as any other because it connects the past to the future. When we think of history as something involving us, suddenly the past becomes colorful, and the discipline finds new and exciting meaning.

Every pastor must become a church historian because he is part of the history he is studying. Like the minister who familiarizes himself with the local history of his church, every pastor must also familiarize himself with the *universal* history of his church—a history that is recorded in biographies, commentaries, letters, diaries, sermons, and writings. Your congregation is connected to a long line of congregations that are spread across continents and cultures, centuries and seas. To ignore your brothers and sisters is to ignore the Christ in whom "all things hold together" (Col. 1:17 NIV).

Another way to avoid the temptation of archaism is to recalibrate our understanding of literature. Books are far more than ink and paper. Instead, they are the packaging of wisdom from the past. To read is to enter into a marvelous and miraculous dialogue with someone in the past—a conversation untouched by time, space, and even death. Without a single word vocally uttered, books become the timeless conduit for wisdom and warnings, encouragements and inspiration. That is why a theological library, no matter how large or small, should always accompany the ministry of the pastor. Libraries are where the dead can speak to the living.

> *The pastor has a vested interest in writing because God is a writer. When you write, you participate in the creative impulse of the Almighty.*

Charles Spurgeon, the most popular preacher in the nineteenth century, labored over words. By the end of his life in 1892, he had published more words in the English language than any preacher in history: dozens of volumes of sermons, one hundred and fifty books, a commentary on Psalms that took twenty years to complete, and a monthly magazine. Spurgeon often preached ten times per week and spent hours painstakingly redacting his sermons for publication. Listen to what he once declared to his congregation:

> *You* need to read. Renounce as much as you will all light literature, but study as much as possible sound theological works, especially the Puritanic writers, and expositions of the Bible. We are quite persuaded that the very best way for you to be spending your leisure, is to be either reading or praying. You

may get much instruction from books which afterwards you may use as a true weapon in your Lord and Master's service.[2]

Spurgeon believed God uses reading to sharpen and improve our effectiveness in ministry, even on a lay level. How essential, then, that pastors be well-read concerning the Bible, theology, church history, and other disciplines.

But pastors should be more than readers; they should be writers, too. There are numerous practical reasons to argue for this, not least being the fact that pastors are those who receive words *from* God through Scripture so they can transmit words *for* God to their hearers. And this being their main task, they ought to become better and better at it. A pastor has been "called" to this ministry (*vocation* comes from the Latin meaning "to call or summon"), and writing is a wonderful way of answering the call.

> *Church history reminds us of our smallness, which wards off pride, and our togetherness, which wards off isolation.*

There is also a theological reason pastors should contribute to church history as writers. As Christians who are made in the image of God and remade in the image of Jesus Christ, the pastor has a vested interest in writing because *God is a writer*. When you write, you participate in the creative impulse of the Almighty. Over the course of centuries, God has—through human agency—written, published, and printed a Book in which He discloses who He is, what He has done, and what He is planning to do. The pastor speaks for God not only with his pulpit but also with his pen.

And keep in mind: ministry is never myopic. Instead, it expands beyond the borders of our churches. Death itself cannot touch the writing minister, for God may use your words to edify congregations not yet born.

Sectarianism

A second challenge to the task of being a pastor-historian is *sectarianism*—that is, the temptation to think that my own church, my own denomination, or my own tradition is the only one that really matters. As believers in Christ whose consciences are held captive to the Word of God, we *have* had, *will* have, and *should* have differing perspectives on secondary doctrinal convictions. That is what makes the church, as Paul wrote in Ephesians 3:10, a display of God's "manifold [*polypoikilos*, 'multilayered' or 'multicolorful,' like Joseph's coat of many colors] wisdom." A monochrome Christianity was never Christ's intent. Church history regulates our unity in Jesus Christ and liberates us to remain denominationally distinctive while also fulfilling Jesus' prayer in John 17:21, "that they may all be one." Church history reminds us of our smallness, which wards off pride, and our togetherness, which wards off isolation.

Jesus Christ did not intend His church to end in the first century with the deaths of His disciples. Quite the opposite. Through them Christ poured a foundation wide enough to support the weight of the apostolic church, your church, and all the churches in between. Jesus Himself was the foundation: "For no one can lay a foundation other than that which is laid, which is Jesus Christ" (1 Cor. 3:11). Church history reveals the fulfillment of Christ's promise to Peter: "On this rock I will build my church" (Matt. 16:18 NIV).

Like the multicolored layers of a grand cathedral, the history of the church is the story of the bones and "living stones" (1 Peter

2:5) on which you and I now stand. Therefore, the pastor should always be aiming in three directions: *down* at what God has built in the past, *around* at what God is building in the present, and *up* at what God will build in the future. Church history removes the temptation of sectarianism by grounding us on the rock of ages—the gospel confession—upon which Christ builds His church.

Presentism

A third challenge to the task of the pastor-historian is *presentism*, which may be described as the prioritization and idolization of the *here* and *now* while neglecting the *there* and *then*. The temptation is an old one, actually; it's pride and the elevation of self. It's shortsighted, too, because by ignoring what God has accomplished in the past, we may not be aware of what He is trying to accomplish in the present.

It is often said that pastors should preach with a Bible in one hand and a newspaper in the other. Is that not enough? The answer is both yes and no. In his preaching, the pastor should certainly be interested in applying the ancient text to modern culture. However, it's not as if God has been twiddling His thumbs in the time between the Bible and our newspapers. In fact, between the first century and the twenty-first century, God has been up to *a lot*. Through the power of His Word and the presence of His Spirit, God has been "making all things new" (Rev. 21:5). Between the early church and the present church, Christ has been working in the gaps—working to free slaves from spiritual bondage, working to inform, reform, and transform His holy church, and working to fulfill that ancient promise declared to Abraham, "I will surely bless you and make your descendants as numerous as the stars in the sky" (Gen. 22:17 NIV). *You* were represented as one of those stars. Sandwiched between the Bible and the newspaper is a galaxy of sinners just like us whose souls have been made to shine because of the undeserved righteousness Christ imputed. Indeed, the lights of those throughout history have something to teach us about how we, too, can "let [our] light shine before others" (Matt. 5:16 NIV).

To ignore church history is to ignore God's activity in this world. But to embrace and teach it is to continue the lifesaving story of God's ongoing mission. Church history is how we remember who we are. It reminds us where we have been. And it helps us follow God where He is leading.

We often think of Jonathan Edwards as the greatest theologian America has ever produced. And to be sure, he was not less than that. But he was also more than that. As great a preacher, philosopher, artist, and mathematician as he was, Jonathan Edwards was also a church historian. His last great work, which he did not finish, was a history book entitled *The History of the Work of Redemption*. Yet little could Edwards know the immense encouragement his earlier work, *The Life and Diary of David Brainerd*, would have upon the future. (Brainerd was a missionary to the Native Americans who died at the age of 29 in 1747.) Fifty years after his death, Brainerd's biography encouraged William Carey, who ministered to Hindus in India. One hundred and fifty years later, Brainerd's biography had become a staple in American literature. Two hundred years later, a young Wheaton student named Jim Elliot would pick up Brainerd's biography and find encouragement for his ministry in Ecuador. The transmission of church history has often been the means through which the gospel of Jesus Christ reaches the dark and dying world.

There are other benefits of church history. It encourages us to continue in ministry in the midst of suffering, loss, rejection, and persecution. It presents a cornucopia of Christians who have survived life's fiercest storms. It reminds us we are not alone in our struggles, and in the same way that others have overcome their obstacles by clinging to Jesus Christ, we too shall overcome. Additionally, church history nourishes us with libraries of devotional literature that replenishes our hearts and refreshes our minds. It keeps alive the memories of brave but ordinary people who feared God more than man and surrendered everything for the sake of the gospel, even when it cost them the loss of reputation and life.

Church history also holds us accountable to God, and to one another, by reminding us that we are part of "a great cloud of witnesses" (Heb. 12:1). We are in the company of past and future believers who faithfully stewarded their resources, platforms, finances, and ministries and embodied John 3:30: "[Christ] must increase, but I must decrease" (KJV). Church history guards our doctrine by holding us accountable to the Word of God as it was hammered out through the consensus of orthodox Christianity. Church history also puts us in touch with our spiritual genealogy and reminds us that we are not alone on this pilgrimage.

The task of the pastor-historian is not to reinvent the wheel, but to keep it spinning for new generations. It is better to be faithful than original. Originality, in fact, is usually the bedrock of heresy. Faithfulness is our ultimate aim—faithfulness in transmitting the victorious story of salvation and the "faith that was once for all entrusted to God's holy people" (Jude 1:3 NIV).

How to Implement Church History

There are a few practical ways to incorporate church history into your life, family, and ministry. First of all, forget building a man cave and invest instead in a theological library. You are a pilgrim, not a tourist. Allocate a portion of your personal budget or church budget to purchasing commentaries, biographies, sermons, and devotionals. You need the past more than you know—more, even, than your deacons or elders know. Carve out space in your house, in your office, and in your calendar for studying what God has accomplished in the past.

Read church history regularly to your family. Every Sunday evening, Eliza Spurgeon gave her son Charles one of the greatest gifts by reading to him and his siblings selections from Richard Baxter's *Call to the Unconverted.* Eliza had a marvelous ministry in pointing her children to the wisdom, bravery, and boldness of the past, and in doing so she was also pointing Charles forward. On January 4, 1859, after five years of full-time Christian ministry, Charles Spurgeon offered the following words to the Young Men's Christian Association at Exeter Hall: "Oh, that I could have the Spirit of God in me, till I was filled with it to the brim, that I might always feel as Baxter did when he said,— 'I preached as never sure to preach again, and as a dying man to dying men.'"[3]

Another way to implement church history in your ministry is to mark off one month per year ("I Love History Month," perhaps) dedicated to the preaching of God's Word in light of Christian heroes. Sunday-school classes are also ideal venues for leading congregations deeper into more interactive discussions about the

You will contribute to what the future needs to know by first learning what the past has to say.

history of the church. Incorporating examples from church history into your sermons adds richness to your preaching. Reading how others handled (or mishandled) God's Word will sharpen your own treatment of the text. You are not the first steward of Scripture, nor will you be the last. You will contribute to what the future needs to know by first learning what the past has to say.

Intentionally integrating church history into the life of your church will produce greater sensitivity to doctrinal and confessional convictions. It motivates congregations to participate in social ministry opportunities. It offers youth groups godly examples of Christian heroism, sacrifice, and selflessness and urges them to live without regret or retreat. It comforts the elderly by reminding them of those who have loved and served Christ faithfully to the end. Church history also expands the perspective of leaders and teachers by encouraging them to seek and find truth wherever it is found (see Heb. 3:7–19). Church history solicits deeper devotion to Jesus Christ by arming and equipping the church with centuries of spiritual literature. It also brings your congregation into greater contact and cooperation with other churches in your community, helping you stand together as torchbearers casting light and life against the temptations of the world, the flesh, and the devil.

B. H. Carroll once said, "The great crying want of this day in our churches is fire."[4] Is that your desire? Do you long for spiritual heat in your own heart, in your family, in your congregation, and in your city, country, and world? Do we yearn for national revival to spread across our land as it once did through the ministries of Jonathan Edwards, George Whitefield, and John Wesley?

God is still in the business of sending fire. His flames still flicker. Bushes still burn. As Carl F. H. Henry once wrote, "The living God is the God who speaks."[5] The Holy One is not hoarse. "I have indeed seen the misery of my people in Egypt. I have heard them crying out because of their slave drivers, and I am concerned about their suffering" (Ex. 3:7 NIV). That message is as true today as it was when Moses heard it. God's heart still beats for the wounded of this world. Yahweh still rescues slaves from captivity. He still leads the way into the wilderness. The Jews brought Joseph's lifeless body on their journey, but we have someone better to carry: the *risen Christ*! One day, as Tolkien's third and final title in the series reminds us, there will be *The Return of the King*, whose eyes, as John said on Patmos, "are like a flame of fire" (Rev. 19:12). On that day, Christ will lead His pilgrims home, and a new chapter—a better chapter— of church history will begin, somewhere over the rainbow.

Pastor as Evangelist

— *John Mark Yeats* —

I f the numbers hold true, evangelism has fallen on hard times. Look at the latest report from your denomination or association of churches. In the Southern Baptist Convention, one of the ways we measure evangelism is through the number of people taking the first step of obedience in following Christ through baptism. As recently as 2014, the denomination informed their churches that nearly ten thousand Southern Baptist churches did not baptize a single person that year.[1]

No one can miss the alarm bells ringing. How could it be that the Southern Baptists—once well-known for fervent evangelism—could be missing the mark so widely that almost a quarter of their congregations did not stir the waters of their baptistery?

Let's zoom in even further. In a Baptist association in northwest Missouri near where I teach, there are a total of forty-three participating churches. Out of those forty-three churches, only one hundred and seventy baptisms were reported last year. That's 3.95 people per congregation. This isn't overwhelming or overly inspiring. While we could look at quite a few causes for that low number, like shrinking rural populations or demographics, what is more telling is that out of those forty-three churches, 35 percent of them reported absolutely *zero* baptisms.[2]

This is unsettling on many levels. The blame game continues to circulate on this issue, with voices attacking specific soteriological concepts, application of specific types of ecclesiology, preaching trends, or even the people in the pew. Culturally, it may take longer to see a person come to faith, but the radical drop in numbers suggests something much more dire. It suggests that our congregations have lost their love for the lost, their love for sharing the gospel, and, dare we say it, their first love: Jesus.

Regardless of factors, a significant conversation must take place about pastors and their role as lead evangelists within their congregations. As pastors, the gospel is our business. We have the privilege of speaking, teaching, and sharing the hope of Jesus daily, not just on Sunday mornings. In the midst of the broader battles found in the shifting of Western culture, pastors should be on the front lines leading congregants into the conflict. If congregational leadership matters, the portrait of the pastor as lead evangelist must become an essential, biblical framework that shapes our understanding of pastoral ministry. Pastors *must* be engaged in the work of evangelism, apply the text to the issue at hand, and then turn and give some practical help for living out a life of evangelism in the ministry context of the local church.

What Does It Mean for a Pastor to Be an Evangelist?

We can all make the excuses. We may be introverts, serve in incredibly difficult ministry contexts, or have any other number of challenges. But no matter how you slice it, pastors are the lead evangelists in every congregation. Regardless of what else may be in your job description, you are *the* evangelist for the people who gather at your church. They look to you for direction in understanding the Scriptures. They observe you and your family as they set standards in their own lives for following Christ. If your personal life fails to model a Christianity that upholds evangelism as a priority, it will continue to be a weakness in the ministry of your local church. What do they learn from your life about the nature of the gospel and sharing the good news?

One of the pastors I served under in my earliest days of ministry, Mac, made certain I understood the importance of modeling consistent evangelism to the youth I served. Whether it is on a ski lift in Colorado, on a beach on the Gulf Coast, or at a restaurant, we have divine opportunities with every person we meet. For the students I was mentoring, this meant opportunities to push beyond the veil of awkwardness to show how natural conversations about spiritual matters can take place with people. Mac eventually went on to plant his own congregation that experienced radical growth, most of which occurred through his investment in evangelism and then teaching others to do the same.

Mac cautioned us that the "default" mode of many church leaders is "come and see." This approach features a pastor placing the weight of his duty on teaching gospel truth from the platform. While gospel proclamation from the text of Scripture is an essential component of preaching, Mac argued that to make this the sole or main evangelistic output for us as pastors is to fall short of the claims that Scripture places on our lives.

Why Should a Pastor Also Be an Evangelist?

To answer this question, let's examine what Scripture says before we move to practical applications of the text. We will look at three texts: the Great Commission (Matt. 28:18–20), the Divine Mandate (Acts 1:6–8), and the Great Sending (Matt. 10).

The Great Commission

And Jesus came and said to them, "All authority in heaven and on earth has been given to me. Go therefore and make disciples of all nations, baptizing them in the name of the Father and of the Son and of the Holy Spirit, teaching them to observe all that I have commanded you. And behold, I am with you always, to the end of the age." (Matt. 28:18–20)

> *Ben committed not to eat dinner with his family until he had shared the gospel with at least one person that day. That may have meant a late return from work, but as he established the pattern, Ben recounted the hundreds of people who had heard the gospel through his faithfulness in sharing it over a lifetime.*

The core idea of the Great Commission is the replication of the Jesus movement. Thus, the central command in the text is to "disciple" or "make disciples." In the same way Jesus called His disciples, we are to do the same for others. The process is rather simple: invite people to follow Jesus, help them grow in Jesus' teachings, and then repeat. The progression of following Jesus into deeper levels of commitment becomes overtly clear.

However, no one hears unless we go. Whether this is understood as a command—"Go!"—or more organically—"As you are going"—the weight of the text still forces the hearer to reconcile that we have a responsibility to let the nations hear about the Savior.[3] For ethnocentric Jews of the Second Temple Period, this had to be the hardest component of Jesus' command. They could train. They could baptize. But going to the nations? This concept stretched the limits of received tradition. The nations were to see the truth of Judaism primarily through the lived life of the community. In this way, they were the "light for the nations" (Isa. 49:6). There was no necessity to "go." But "going" is exactly what we are commanded to do. The message of the gospel is for all. Thus, we go. As pastor-evangelists, do we make this an attendant portion of our personal schedule?

When I met Ben, I sat and listened to story after story about how God changed the lives of hundreds through his work as a businessman. During an early period of his life, Ben made a commitment with his wife, his pastor, and the church. Ben committed not to eat dinner with his family until he had shared the gospel with at least one person that day. That may have meant a late return from work, but as he established the pattern, Ben recounted the hundreds of people who had heard the gospel through his faithfulness in sharing it over a lifetime.

What if, like Ben, more pastors had serious commitments to strategically engage the lost in their communities? And lest we forget as we head out the door, the entire Great Commission hinges on the established authority Christ possesses, not our personal skills of persuasion. Nothing on earth will thwart His plan. This commissioning that we share is tied to His power as He deputizes us to be His agents of the gospel. But we never go alone. He promises His presence as we fulfill His will.

The Divine Mandate

> So when they had come together, they asked him, "Lord, will you at this time restore the kingdom to Israel?" He said to them, "It is not for you to know times or seasons that the Father has fixed by his own authority. But you will receive power when the Holy Spirit has come upon you, and you will be my witnesses in Jerusalem and in all Judea and Samaria, and to the end of the earth." (Acts 1:6–8)

Similar to the Great Commission, Jesus tells His disciples to be those who testify boldly throughout the world about the good news of the gospel. He reminds them that the timing of the kingdom is not an issue they should be concerned about. Instead, as recipients of the gospel, they should be witnesses to the gospel throughout the world. The clear implication is the indiscriminate sowing of the gospel message within local areas (Jerusalem), regional enclaves (Judea and Samaria), and around the world. These concentric circles of gospel influence and advance ensure the spreading of Jesus' message to every tribe, nation, and tongue (Rev. 7:9).

As with the Great Commission, our divine mandate also arrives with divine power—this time from the presence of the Holy Spirit. This same Spirit of God that raised Jesus from the dead (see Rom. 8:11) empowers believers to become powerful witnesses to the truth of the risen Christ. As pastor-evangelists, our mandate is simple: get out there as witnesses! As we accomplish the gospel mandate, we enlist all believers in following the command of God to reach the world for Christ.

The Great Sending

Matthew 10 frames an account of Jesus equipping His disciples to do the work of ministry (see also Mark 6:7–14 and Luke 9:1–10). Jesus teaches them, warns them, and subsequently sends them out. This training from the Chief Shepherd of Israel to the disciples to go to the "lost sheep of . . . Israel" (v. 6) marks the plan of the Savior to utilize leaders in the church to be key workers in evangelism. The disciples are told explicitly, "Proclaim as you go, saying, 'The kingdom of heaven is at hand'" (Matt. 10:7). Despite the challenges they will surely face, they are not to shirk from the challenge. They are to go.[4]

After Jesus' ascension, the disciples latch on to this model. We see the pattern continue in the book of Acts as the apostles preach the gospel in public and share in private. Paul encourages his protégé Timothy to "be ready in season and out of season" (2 Tim. 4:2). Even Jesus made sure that His disciples knew that the "fields are white for harvest" (John 4:35). The early Christians were on the move evangelistically—they were fervent, willing, and ready.

While we cannot escape that this command to go encompasses all believers, do we as pastors actually model the commands of Christ to our people? If we take the claims of Scripture seriously, we need to be confident and active in living the life of a pastor-evangelist.

How Then Should We Share?

The Scriptures are clear about the priority of evangelism in our congregations, and we must move beyond the mental assent of the claims of evangelism, which are all too simple to embrace. As I often tell my students, orthodoxy begets orthopraxy. In other words, if we hold to right belief about the nature of the gospel and about its demands and claims on our lives, we will move to action. Right belief demands right action.

As we look to the role of the pastor-evangelist as the leader of the church's evangelism activities, how can we create rightly ordered behaviors in our own lives? There are at least seven ideas worth pursuing as we serve our congregations in this way.

Make evangelism an essential priority

Historian Michael Green researched the evangelistic patterns of the early church and discovered how the first generations after Christ's death, burial, and resurrection understood the concept of evangelism. For pastors seeking to lead congregations in tumultuous cultural circumstances, there is no better example than that of the first three centuries of the Christian church. During that period, Christians experienced unbelievable pressure from a government that oscillated from apathy to outright hatred. Even with formidable cultural opposition, these same believers saw the gospel blossom and become the dominant religion in the West.

Part of this growth, Green argues, is because evangelism permeated the very essence of life in the early Christian community. In *Evangelism in the Early Church*, Green writes, "One of the most notable impressions the literature of the first and second century made upon me as I wrote this book was the sheer passion of these early Christians!"[5] Specifically, Green outlines four key priorities that the church projected relating to evangelism.

First, evangelism primarily happened *outside* of the church. The idea of passive evangelism or a "Come and see" methodology didn't exist. The close quarters of the urban setting in many contexts allowed for believers to take the gospel everywhere as they were living their life. Evangelism happened in the street, while washing clothes, during work, and in many other loci of life itself. The church's externally focused mission saw clear results.

The passion for evangelism outside the church was joined with a personal boldness to share the gospel verbally. This second priority of evangelism, according to Green, pushed the message beyond a lifestyle witness to a verbal proclamation of the Christian message. If "faith comes from hearing" (Rom. 10:17), these Christians wanted to be certain as many people as possible heard the message of the gospel.

Third, Green argues, Christians used hospitality in their homes for "gossiping the gospel."[6] Believers would ask "Did you hear?" style questions to encourage neighbors and others to connect to the truth of the gospel message. This form of gossip allowed the believer to test the hearer's receptivity while still positing the truth of the gospel message.

Fourth, the role of the life of the Holy Spirit in the believer's life was one of the greatest motivations for evangelism that Christians carried. If the power of God was with them, then they could trust God would see them through to the end. They didn't need to worry about the future or even tomorrow, for their King held their life in His capable hands.

Connect evangelism with the tension of eschatology

When looking at the priorities of the early church, we see a clear undergirding of appropriate apocalyptic tension. *When would Jesus return? Would the cultural moment shift and therefore make it harder to share the gospel? How can we make the most of this moment for Christ?* As Christians studied the writings of Scripture, they emphasized the imminent return of Christ. This heightened urgency provoked many Christians to share their faith during those first few centuries.

In the revivals of the late 1970s, evangelicals, much like the early church, were overwhelmingly convinced that the return of Christ was imminent. Movies like *A Thief in the Night* made sure you did not even sleep before dealing with the salvation of your soul. End-times fever driven by dispensational interpretation aided in the task of evangelism, too, because pastors and people truly believed the end was nigh. There was a fear that every person we knew may miss out on eternity with God when He appeared the very next moment. Early Contemporary Christian musician Larry Norman penned the passionate plea,

> I wish we'd all been ready.
> I wish we'd all been ready.
> There's no time to change your mind;
> The Son has come and you've been left behind.[7]

The fear was simple: If Jesus returns today, are the people we know and love ready to meet Jesus at the judgment seat? Would they know Christ fully? I'm not advocating everything about these eschatologies, but the Scriptures are crystal clear about the imminent physical return of Christ and the coming judgment. Pastors, more than anyone else, should feel the weight of the eschatological reality that Jesus is coming soon! There is limited time for us to work in the fields before us.

Make evangelism a key component of your discipleship trajectory

There was a season in my pastoral ministry when almost every Wednesday night my pastoral interns or other lay people would hit the road with me to follow up on those who had visited on Sunday. The primary reason for this visit was evangelistic. We often had no idea about the spiritual state of the people who had come into our building on Sunday, and this provided the perfect opportunity to share Christ with them. Of course, having fellow church members along for the ride meant I had the opportunity for one-on-one or one-on-two discipleship.

This took a shift in the church calendar. Instead of teaching yet another Bible study on Wednesday night, I encouraged another adult to teach those who weren't volunteering with children or youth ministries, and I led a group of members to meet with people outside the doors of the church for over an hour.

On those nights, we not only visited our intended contacts, but we would go to the local park or some other area and chat with people about the gospel. We had great conversations with people of other faiths, atheists, and those who had walked away from their faith. This fruitful time week after week allowed me to see growth and discipleship in so many men as they grew in their personal abilities to share the gospel with others. When we added this to the regular work we were doing outside of our doors with refugees, school districts, and the chamber of commerce, we began to see some amazing growth in our people and the church. Pastor-evangelists must find ways to make evangelism a strategic part of the schedule and life of the church.

One way to do this is to set clear expectations for your church staff, elders, and deacons relating to evangelism. Without clearly articulating what that standard should be, your people may not prioritize evangelism in the midst of all the other duties they fulfill for the congregation. An evangelistic church is led by people passionate about evangelism in every area of the life of the congregation. If you lead in this way, all ministries stay focused on the main thing! Even new-members classes, marriage-counseling sessions, and service opportunities all become part of the congregation's means of reaching the lost with the gospel!

Preach the Word faithfully and evangelistically

I would guess that most pastor-evangelists treasure preaching more than almost every other aspect of ministry. We enjoy the opportunity to expound the Word of God weekly. This privilege and honor of sharing the Bible is a component of our calling and an essential ingredient in congregational discipleship. As we unpack the words of the text, we do so carefully to bring honor to God and feed the souls of those gathered.

But for all of our study and exposition, we should never forget the focus of our preaching: the risen Savior. Consequently, we must preach evangelistically, calling people to repentance. The Spirit of God does His work in the hearts of the people as we communicate the riches of the gospel.

True evangelistic preaching communicates the truths of the gospel throughout. It does not simply teach the text and then "tack on" the gospel message. We consistently and faithfully point people to the Savior as we preach the whole counsel of God. As we highlight the nature of the gospel, we call people to respond to the demands of the text. Don't let up. Call sinners to repent and believers to walk with their Savior.

This also means giving space and opportunity for responding to the message. In many instances, a moment of response should be given at the conclusion of the sermon. This may be a time for prayer and reflection or even a full invitation. Never manipulate this time, but do not rush the movement of the Spirit of God, either. Even when concluding the sermon, always mention opportunities for further discussion. For those who are far from God, this may be essential to them coming to faith at a later date. It was through post-sermon interaction and dialogue with Ambrose of Milan that Augustine eventually came to faith—over the course of a couple years of discussion.

Create evangelistic small groups

There was a time in evangelicalism that Sunday school and small-group Bible studies were the means by which churches saw incredible growth. Each group encouraged the participants to invite family members, friends, and neighbors to come be a part of a smaller gathering of believers. Through the ongoing care of those in attendance, coupled with appropriate discipleship materials, one by one people came to faith in Christ. Additionally, each group continued to pray strategically for the lost in their community and specifically for the names of individuals who didn't know Christ. This discipline worked through the entire ethos of the church, creating a community driven by evangelism.

It takes a bold pastor to lead out in this type of small-group structure and to see success in these groups. If a congregation is willing to make the investment, you begin to see the changes that can only come as the members of the congregation participate in the process of evangelism.

As a pastor-evangelist, equipping your people to live out the gospel in a community that's passionate about seeing the lost saved is transformative. In many ways, it creates new synergies for organic discipleship relationships that bear fruit over and over again. To truly launch this level of discipleship, lead a small group in the community that carries these same values. Otherwise, this becomes another "Do as I say, not as I do" reality. As you lead and your group grows, use it to launch other new evangelistic groups. This becomes the opportunity to train the next leaders as you go and to empower them to reach others with the gospel.

Lead like a missionary

Every missionary serves in a specific context. Give any missionary a year in the field and they can tell you the dynamics of the cultural leadership. They will know the demographics and will have created strategic plans to engage that region.

In our modern, post-Christian society, pastors must be on the front lines of thinking and leading missiologically. How well do you know your community? How engaged are you in the cultural markers of your mission field to the extent you are able? Do you know where people gather, relax, and work? How are you engaging the leaders in the community? How is your church reaching into the lives of families who live in the area?

I like to think of the 1-3-5 principle of effective engagement. Your congregation should know and be well known by people within a one-mile radius. These are the individuals God has specifically given you to reach. To be sure, your congregants may come from further away, but God has given you neighbors to engage. Your energy should be focused on the homes, businesses, and organizations in that target range.

As you work diligently in the one-mile radius, you begin to move outward in concentric circles of three miles and five miles to engage the culture centers of that broader field. Identify the schools and sports fields that comprise the hub of life for families in your community. Discover ways to serve those who gather there and build relationships, eventually sharing the gospel with them. These gospel-oriented relationships matter for reaching the lost and engaging them with the good news of Jesus.

In his book *The Rise of Christianity*, sociologist Rodney Stark analyzed the rapid growth of the early church. He framed his study by questioning how an obscure movement from a remote territory became the dominant religion in the West. His research challenges leading assumptions about how evangelism works within a given cultural context.

"Evangelists assume that doctrinal appeal lies at the heart of the conversion process—that people hear the message, find it attractive, and embrace the faith," writes Stark. However, his research reveals that personal relationships are actually the largest factor in the growth of any religious group. "The basis for successful conversionist movements is growth through social networks, through a *structure of direct and intimate interpersonal attachments.*"[8] In other words, those personal relationships matter! We should be building them continually. Apologetics may be effective, but for all the people who fear evangelism due to a lack of apologetic training, they should take a deep breath and reengage. Every person can make a difference by building a relationship and sharing the gospel.

Stark never argues that doctrine doesn't matter; rather, he says that when we underplay the role of personal relationships, we miss connecting people with the gospel. These relationships matter in the life of the congregation as a whole and can be the leading factor in making long-term disciples of people who come to faith in Christ.

There is a danger with this relational approach, however,

which is that often those relationships grow and connect so well that we forget to continue to forge new ones. Stark continues, "Most new religious movements fail because they quickly become closed, or semiclosed networks. That is, they fail to keep forming and sustaining attachments to outsiders and thereby lose the capacity to grow."[9] The cliché "holy huddle" exists for a reason—it is our natural inclination to group with like-minded people and stave off outsiders. But healthy Christian communities don't do this. They stay outward facing even as they enjoy distinctly Christian fellowship.

Your role as a pastor-evangelist is to be part-missionary, to know how to read the community God has given to your church. Define it. Build maps. Get engaged in the lives of the people who live there. If every pastor would utilize the wealth of demographic and analytical tools available to congregations, it could be a game-changer for evangelism, mission reach, and casting a biblical vision for the area God has given to your congregation.

I've seen schools transformed, cities changed, and new churches started all because a pastor-evangelist encouraged his people to pursue the lost. And it always starts with prayer.

Be a church that prays for the lost

One of the best barometers of the spiritual health of a congregation is its prayer life, specifically whether it prays for the lost. If congregations are only worried about lifting up their own needs, they have lost their focus on the broader mission they are called to accomplish. Charles Spurgeon put it this way: "Remember that prayer is effectual with God. . . . We ought to bestir ourselves for men's souls, and we cannot do better for them than by praying for them."[10] How frequently in your own devotional time do you pray for the lost? When was the last time you trained your people how to do the same? Does your church pray corporately for the lost?

Amazingly, as we pray God inevitably raises men and women in our congregations to creatively engage the lost. This becomes part of the "train-and-release" method. Teach your people how to reach out to non-Christians, but don't try to micromanage the process. Allow your people to use their giftings to engage the lost, and work with them to effectively accomplish the task. I've seen schools transformed, cities changed, and new churches started all because a pastor-evangelist encouraged his people to pursue the lost. And it always starts with prayer.

Around the year 231, Gregory and his brother escorted their sister to the city of Caesarea in Israel. Gregory had no intent to stay, but while in the city he met the pastor of the church there—an encounter that would change his life forever.

Origen, the famed theologian and preacher of Caesarea, challenged Gregory and his thinking with the gospel. Eventually, Gregory came to trust Christ and was baptized in the church. Origen continued to disciple Gregory until it was determined he could pastor on his own, and then he sent him back to his hometown.

When Gregory arrived back home, he found seventeen Christians attempting to remain faithful despite a hostile culture. Gregory led these Christians to boldly practice their faith while engaging the broader culture. Throughout the course of his thirty years of ministry in that town, Gregory led his people to do all they could to reach the lost. Despite the trials of the Decian persecutions in 250, which were followed in 253 by an outbreak of plague and military encroachment by the Goths, Gregory continued to lead his people to follow Jesus. By the end of his life in 270, Gregory and his congregation had grown significantly, and—so the story goes—only seventeen pagans remained.

This is the challenge: are we willing to lead as pastor-evangelists in our congregations with the hope of seeing men and women commit their lives to Jesus Christ? As pastors, there can be no greater joy or honor. As we serve in the role of pastor-evangelist, we have the privilege of seeing the kingdom of God advance as we await the return of our Savior.

Pastor as Missionary

— *Jason G. Duesing* —

Four years after sending William Carey to India, the Baptist
Missionary Society sent John Fountain to aid Carey and send back
a report. Here's an excerpt from the report, dated November 1796:

> [Carey] labours in the translation of the Scriptures, and has
> nearly finished the New Testament, being somewhere around
> the middle of Revelations. *He keeps the grand end in view*,
> which first induced him to leave his country, and those Chris-
> tian friends he still dearly loves.[1]

He Keeps the Grand End in View

William Carey, a modern missionary pioneer who endured
much hardship, persevered in faithfulness and worldwide influence until the age of seventy-three. How did he manage local,
everyday challenges while maintaining a heart to reach the world?

As Fountain observed, from his earliest days of missionary activity until the end of his life Carey kept the grand end in view.

So what is this grand end?

While it is right to say that the entire Bible points to and reveals the grand end, I believe there is one verse that sums it up well. In Galatians 3:8, the apostle Paul says, "And the Scripture, foreseeing that God would justify the Gentiles by faith, preached the gospel beforehand to Abraham, saying, 'In you shall all the nations be blessed.'" Here Paul explains that God has always had the salvation of the nations in mind. From the beginning, He conveyed to Abraham His plan. In what is often considered the centerpiece of the first five books of the Bible, God says to Abraham,

> Go from your country and your kindred and your father's house to the land that I will show you. And I will make of you a great nation, and I will bless you and make your name great, so that you will be a blessing. I will bless those who bless you, and him who dishonors you I will curse, and in you all the families of the earth shall be blessed. (Gen. 12:1–3)

At the age of seventy-five, Abraham obeyed God, and he and his wife left their country. After a period of travel and time, God met with Abraham, took him outside, and said, "Look toward heaven, and number the stars, if you are able to number them" (Gen. 15:5). The passage continues, "Then [God] said to him, 'So shall your offspring be.' And he believed the LORD, and he counted it to him as righteousness" (vv. 5–6).

After Abraham believed, God made a covenant with him promising that he would be "the father of a multitude of nations" (Gen. 17:4). Paul tells us in Galatians 3:8 that in this event the gospel was preached to Abraham. We might think, "How is this possible, as the name of Jesus Christ is not mentioned?"

What was the gospel preached to Abraham? In short, the gospel preached to Abraham was God's promise to him that through Abraham and his offspring all the nations would be blessed—or simply, that Gentiles, non-Israelites, would be justified by faith.

In Romans 4, Paul explains, "The purpose was to make him [Abraham] the father of all who believe," and, "The words 'it was counted to him' were not written for his sake alone, but for ours also. It will be counted to us who believe in him who raised from the dead Jesus our Lord, who was delivered up for our trespasses and raised for our justification" (Rom. 4:11, 23–25).

The gospel has always had the doctrine of justification at its center. Reconciliation of sinful humanity to a holy God, and the removal of His just condemnation, is the core of gospel truth. Yet to be gospel-centered is to recognize that the gospel was intended for Abraham in the Old-Testament past all the way to you and me in the post–New Testament future. Again, Paul explains that the gospel was "promised beforehand through his prophets in the holy Scriptures, concerning his Son" (Rom. 1:2–3). Or as one twentieth-century poet put it, "Sometimes I think of Abraham / How one star he saw had been lit for me."[2]

The gospel has always contained an intrinsic element of blessing the nations.[3] Because of this, we can say that Muslims and unbelieving Jews are not the true successors to Abraham. Salvation only comes through the One, namely Jesus, in whom this faith is placed and through whom we are justified. And one day, every knee will bow before Him and confess that He is Lord (see Phil. 2:9–10). Until that day, like Carey, we are to keep this grand end in view.

My hope in this chapter is to make one thing clear: the pastor as missionary is the pastor centered on the gospel. The pastor as missionary is not another garment or tool or lens he wears or uses, but rather is the natural, healthy outworking of what it means to have a gospel-centered focus. To explain further what I mean by this, I have three questions to ask and answer:

1. What does a pastor need to know about missions?
2. Why should a pastor be a missionary?
3. How can a pastor most faithfully be a missionary?

What Does a Pastor Need to Know about Missions?

Baseball has long been my sport of choice. In my school-age years, I played other sports with friends in their yards or driveways, but only baseball did I pursue at a competitive level. As a result, it was not until college that I learned the rules of how to play basketball and football. I can remember several weeks when my roommates and I were playing basketball and—aside from knowing I needed to hustle and "get open"—I had no clue what was happening. My teammates would tell me to "run the court" or "block out" or "set a pick," and I stumbled and faked my way along until I learned how to play the game. I was eager to play hard and help my team to win, but I lacked an understanding of the terms for playing.

When it comes to considering the work of the pastor and missions, many of us would be helped to acknowledge that we need a greater understanding of the terms. We know the Great Commission, support and practice evangelism, and even advocate for the missionary task. Yet often the work of missions is like a game we enjoy watching but don't know how to play. Therefore I will present here some basic definitions of several crucial missiological terms. Some of these are elementary and well known, but for the exercise of building a team in which everyone knows the terms and how to play together, I hope you will find this review helpful.

Missionary

John Piper provides a helpful classification of two types of missionaries found in the Bible: the Timothy-type missionary and the Paul-type missionary. He explains, "We call Timothy a missionary because he left home (Lystra, Acts 16:1), joined a traveling team of missionaries, crossed cultures, and ended up overseeing the younger church in Ephesus (1 Tim. 1:3) far from his homeland."[4] The Timothy-type missionary, however, stays on the mission field in the same location even after churches are started and established.

The Paul-type missionary is more itinerant. Paul was "driven by a passion to make God's name known among all the unreached peoples of the world. He never stayed in a place long, once the church was established."[5] The pursuit of traveling to places where there is little to no knowledge of Jesus Christ (Rom. 15:20) distinguishes this type of missionary.

Whether they stay in one place or continue onward to other frontier areas, missionaries are those who cross cultures to share the gospel.

Nations

The Bible records that nations were first created by God in response to the construction of the Tower of Babel (Gen. 11). Previously having one language, the people were dispersed throughout the earth with distinct languages. The nations, both the Jewish nation and all Gentile nations, continue as central entities in God's plan to display His glory and work out salvation and judgment.

It was to the nation of Israel that God sent His Son, Jesus Christ, as Messiah to "suffer and on the third day rise from the dead . . . that repentance for the forgiveness of sins should be proclaimed in his name to *all nations*" (Luke 24:46–47). It is the commission of Christian churches (Matt. 16:18) to continue the task of taking the message of God's plan of salvation (Rom. 10:14–15) to those nations who have not heard (Rom. 15:21). This message will be proclaimed by God's children to the nations until the end of the world (Matt. 24:14). At that time, the Messiah will return to the earth, and all nations will submit to his rule and reign (Phil. 2:10–11). People from every nation will worship him (Rev. 7:9).[6]

Piper helps again here by reminding us that the task of missions is "not just reaching more and more people but more and more peoples—tribes, tongues, peoples, nations." When we understand this biblical definition of the nations (and the prescribed task to reach them), we are encouraged to know that the task of reaching all nations is finishable. "The task is finishable because while the number of individual people keeps growing and changing, the number of people groups (by and large) does not."[7]

Reached and unreached

In Romans 15:19, Paul says, "From Jerusalem and all the way around to Illyricum I have fulfilled the ministry of the gospel of Christ." In 15:23, he explains that he no longer has "any room for work in these regions." What Paul is essentially saying is, "The furthest east I have ever been is Jerusalem, and the furthest west I have ever been is Illyricum. And everywhere in between—in all the places I have been—the ministry has been fulfilled." He has fully preached the gospel of Christ. The idea here is not that every person in that region, as big as it is, is now a Christian. We know that is not the case. But he is saying that all the people in this region *now have access to the gospel.* He has sown seeds, churches have sprouted up, and there are preachers there who will continue the work so that everyone in the region can hear the gospel. The gospel has been preached here, the ministry has been fulfilled, and it's now self-sustaining. In our language today, we would call this region "reached" and "no longer unreached."[8]

In missions, most define a people group as reached when "there is an indigenous church able to evangelize the group."[9] However, there is ongoing discussion about at what point an indigenous church is "able" to evangelize. That is, what percentage of the population needs to be converted in order for that people group to achieve the status of reached? Missiologists Zane Pratt, David Sills, and Jeff Walters, in *Introduction to Global Missions,* follow the common classification of a people group being reached when evangelicals consists of more than 2 percent of the population.[10] However, former missionary and fellow missiologist Robin Hadaway recently argued that setting the reached line at 2 percent is too low and hinders the healthy establishment of churches in a newly reached area. He recommends raising the threshold back to 10 or 20 percent and, along with that, sending more missionaries to areas previously thought of as reached.[11] While that is a fruitful and important discussion, there is at least agreement that people groups with less than 2 percent evangelicals are clearly "unreached."[12]

The 10/40 Window

Unreached people groups exist in just about every country of the world, but they are most concentrated in what's been called the 10/40 Window. Here's a brief explanation of that term:

131

The 10/40 Window is an imaginary box that encloses an area of the globe from 10 degrees north of the equator to 40 degrees north of the equator, and from Northwest Africa to East Asia. Not only does this rectangle contain the majority of the world's unreached lost; it is also home to three major religious blocs: Hinduism, Islam, and Buddhism, as well as areas of greatest poverty.[13]

The 10/40 Window[14]

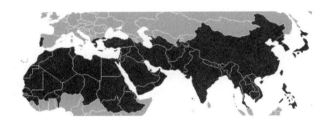

As this region represents such a high concentration of unreached peoples, churches and missionaries rightly focus on the 10/40 Window for preaching the gospel to "those who have never been told" of Jesus (Rom. 15:21).

The Global South

In the later part of the twentieth century, the largest populations of evangelicals around the world started to shift from the historic West to the South. The church is growing rapidly in Latin America, Africa, and parts of Asia. "More Christians live there than in the United States, and they send out more missionaries than the United States and Western Europe."[15] As a result, churches and missionaries in the twenty-first century are increasingly having to adjust their thinking of the West as "reached." Certainly, there are more evangelicals still in the West compared to the 10/40 Window, but the rise of nominal Christianity and the uncertain commitments of the children and grandchildren of evangelicals mean that one day soon, if not already, the churches of the

> *The pastor as missionary means the pastor is a "world Christian" who serves as a model missionary.*

Global South will need to send missionaries to the West.

These are some of the basic terms a pastor should know when it comes to engaging in missions. Together they help us frame our shared task of reaching the world for Christ. They also aid us in considering our next question: "Why should a pastor be a missionary?"

Why Should a Pastor Be a Missionary?

In recent years our family survived our "Angry Birds" season of life. For a period of time our kids could not get enough of this game, to the extent that we even had an Angry Birds birthday party along the way. If you have played this game, you know that the key to advancing is trajectory. How you aim the angry bird makes all the difference for achieving maximum effect. While hopefully avoiding anger, the key for the pastor as missionary is also trajectory. In what direction the pastor points, the church follows.

That said, it isn't enough for a pastor to herald the importance of missions. He must underscore its importance biblically and encourage his people to be *world* Christians. As Tom Stellar explains,

Not every Christian is called to be a missionary, but every follower of Christ is called to be a world Christian. A world Christian is someone who is so gripped by the glory of God and the glory of his global purpose that he chooses to align himself with God's mission to fill the earth with the knowledge of his glory as the waters cover the sea (Hab. 2:14).[16]

The pastor as missionary means the pastor is a "world Christian" who serves as a model missionary. This means he is an exemplar of one who champions the end goal of the gospel and those who take it to the ends of the earth. This is not another hat he must wear but is instead the natural outgrowth of his dedication to the gospel and his desire to see the nations reached.

We come now to why pastors ought to encourage their people to be *globally* minded. Often times, in classrooms or church hallways, well-meaning students or church members ask why it is that we need to emphasize and fund long-range, global mission efforts when there are so many lost people right here at home. This is a question of stewardship and deserves a good answer. There are several reasons why.

First, we should seek the unreached because (as we recently discussed) the Great Commission expects disciples to be made of all people groups—large or small, easy or hard to find, with or without printed languages—all groups. The clear heart of the Bible is for God's people to desire "all the peoples" to praise God and for Him to "let the nations be glad and sing for joy" (Ps. 67:3–4).

Second, the earliest Christians were themselves compelled to take the gospel to where Christ had not yet been named so that "those who have never been told of him will see, and those who have never heard will understand" (Rom. 15:21). The first churches that formed after Pentecost clearly saw the need to carry the good news beyond their local communities. Even though their communities needed the gospel, too, the church organized its ministry with a view of supporting those who were sent to all those yet to hear and understand.

Third is the simple issue of effective use of manpower. When Nehemiah set out to rebuild the wall around Jerusalem, he stationed people in the lowest parts and in the open spaces (Neh. 4:13). He did not stack them all in one part or in one place. When looking to reach the nations with the gospel, yes, sufficient workers should stay and labor in the fields at home, for there is much work to be done, and those traveling to the unreached cannot do so without their support. But more and more workers should also be sent and equipped to reach areas where no work has ever been done. In an earlier century, one missions-minded pastor explained it this way:

> Imagine I was employed by the owner of a vineyard to gather grapes in his vineyard. The general instructions were that as many grapes as possible should be gathered. I went down to the gate of the vineyard and found the area around the walls well plucked and the ground covered with pickers. Yet away off in the distance no pickers at all are in sight and the vines are loaded to the ground. Would I need a special visit and order from the owner of the vineyard to instruct me as to my duty?[17]

The answer is clear: of course not. The areas of greatest neglect are the areas of greatest need.

This analogy bears striking resemblance to worldwide realities today. The Joshua Project documents that there are more Timothy-type missionaries than Paul-type missionaries. More than 90 percent of the global evangelical missionary effort serves among the 60 percent of the world that is reached or within reach.[18] This means that only 10 percent of our missionary force is working among the remaining 40 percent who have never heard the gospel or have little access to it. Further, each year Open Doors International generates their World Watch List to determine the top fifty countries where persecution of Christians for religious reasons is worst. For 2017, the top five countries include North Korea, Somalia, Afghanistan, Pakistan, and Sudan.[19] When you look at that list in light of where the current evangelical missionary force is deployed, we can draw the following conclusion: all of those places are where Christian persecution is greatest, the most people are unreached, and the fewest evangelical missionaries are working. That is an easy-to-see mismatch, and pastors serving in reached areas are in the best position to do something about it.[20]

Why, then, should the pastor be a missionary? So he can help mobilize the church for missions. Often we think that only missionaries should give thought, time, and vision to missions. Our view of the world beyond where we live is often uninformed—truly foreign. We are much like Prince Caspian of Narnia, who asks Edmund, who was from England, "It must be exciting to live on a thing like a ball. Have you ever been to the parts where people walk about upside-down?"[21]

Yet the call to serve and reach those who have not heard requires only qualified messengers, not an extra command or calling from God. Jesus Christ has already said to make disciples of all nations (Matt. 28:19), and there are many nations who have not heard His name.

As model missionaries, pastors should lead their churches to go and to support the ongoing work of Timothy- and Paul-type missionaries all over the globe—especially in the parts most in need of the gospel. To put it another way, as shepherds of churches seeking to fulfill the Great Commission, pastors should lead in seeking and finding people from all the nations that seemingly "walk about upside-down" and help make the task of missions not so foreign.

How Can a Pastor Most Faithfully Be a Missionary?

The apostles established early on what the primary tasks of a pastor include. In Acts 6:4, they explain that pastors are to devote themselves to "prayer and to the ministry of the word." Similar to how all the Law and the Prophets are summarized by the commands to love God and neighbor (Matt 22:36–40), so it is with the work of the pastor in Acts 6:4. While pastors have very diverse day-to-day tasks, in the end they are to focus on prayer and preaching. Therefore, when seeking to answer how the pastor can be a missionary, we are not looking to add an additional line on the job description. The pastor as missionary is a healthy and natural extension of his work in prayer and preaching, not a competition to it.

Prayer

As the pastor leads his congregation in prayer, he should not miss the historic connection between prayer and missions. There are many examples in history of how God's people praying has led to missionary zeal and advance, but one prominent example is that of Jonathan Edwards. During his final years in Northampton, Massachusetts, Edwards received an invitation from Scotland to participate in a concert of prayer as a means of rejuvenating the revivals. Edwards had already come to think of and observe prayer as an appropriate conduit for advancing the remarkable revivals we now call the Great Awakening of the 1730s.

In response to the request, in 1748 Edwards published sermons on Zechariah 8:20–22 entitled *An Humble Attempt*. Edwards's work exhorted many, both in America and Scotland, to "by united and extraordinary prayer, seek to God that he would come and manifest himself, and grant the tokens and fruits of his gracious presence." For, Edwards argued, "the greatest effusion of the Spirit that ever yet has been, even that which was in the primitive times of the Christian church, which began in Jerusalem on the day of Pentecost, was in answer to extraordinary prayer." Edwards saw prayer as "the means of awakening others . . . and disposing them to join with God's people in that extraordinary seeking and serving of God." In Edwards's mind, and rightfully so, prayer was the key to revival and the spread of the gospel.[22]

While Edwards's work had immediate influence, a few decades later *An Humble Attempt* would find even greater significance for the advancement of global missions through pastors praying. In 1784, English pastors Andrew Fuller and William Carey gained access to Edwards's work and read it with eyes primed for rays of hopeful light in the task of taking the gospel to the ends of the earth. As McClymond and McDermott note, "Carey used the *Humble Attempt* to discount the contention that certain prophesies had to be fulfilled before the heathen could be converted." Combined with Edwards's *Life of David Brainerd* (1749) and *Freedom of the Will* (1754), Fuller and Carey found in Edwards a "grandfather" of modern missions.[23] From those in England and America who read Edwards came the London Missionary Society, the Baptist Missionary Society, the Scottish Missionary Society, and the American Board of Commissioners for Foreign Missions.[24] In addition to

Edwards and Carey, there were many others who played a part in the start of the modern missions movement. But the main point is that, following the design of God, organized prayer served as the fuel for missionary advance.

Not only does prayer motivate people for missions, it can also help educate them for missions. For example, pastors can use prayer to help their people become more knowledgeable of geography. Recently, Allison Meier reported that for five centuries a fictional island remained on official maps simply because it was placed there and those tending to the maps were none the wiser—and not so for five hundred years.[25] Often the simple hurdle of geography is one of the hindrances to leading churches to "get their minds around the world." When people are not certain where the people they are praying for are located on a map, the challenges of supporting and serving them only increase. By incorporating missions and geography into the prayer times of the church, the pastor serves the heart and global focus of his congregation well. One of the best ways to do this is the regular use of the resource *Operation World*.[26]

Preaching

As the pastor leads in the ministry of the Word, here, too, he should not miss the opportunity to incorporate a missions focus into his sermons. Throughout history, the practice of preachers including illustrations from the lives of missionaries in their sermons or preaching with a global focus has resulted, as one professor commented, in the dual effect of encouraging those already serving in missions as well as calling many into service.[27] Here are a few ideas for incorporating a missions focus in your sermons.

First, share powerful quotes and stories about missions.

Sometimes the most effective way to make a point or bring to life a figure from history is simply to read a selection from their writings and let them speak for themselves. Of course, the preacher must practice care here; often what we think is powerful when read in our study only seems dull when spoken aloud in a sermon. One text that I read regularly, and have found to carry the intended effect, at least in a classroom setting, is the following selection from William Carey's *An Enquiry into the Obligations of Christians to Use Means for the Conversion of the Heathens* (1792). In this section, Carey is reminding his readers who are called of God to gospel ministry that such a call is sufficient for any global location of service or circumstance to which God might send His servant:

> A Christian minister is a person who in a peculiar sense is not his own; he is the servant of God, and therefore ought to be wholly devoted to him. By entering on that sacred office he solemnly undertakes to be always engaged, as much as possible, in the Lord's work, and not to choose his own pleasure, or employment, or pursue the ministry as a something that is to subserve his own ends, or interests, or as a kind of bye-work. He engages to go where God pleases, and to do, or endure what he sees fit to command, or call him to, in the exercise of his function. He virtually bids farewell to friends, pleasures, and comforts, and stands in readiness to endure the greatest sufferings in the work of his Lord, and Master. . . . Thus the apostles acted, in the primitive times, and endured hardness, as good soldiers of Jesus Christ; and though we living in a civilized country where Christianity is protected by law, are not called to suffer these things while we continue here, yet I question whether all are

justified in staying here, while so many are perishing without means of grace in other lands.

Sure I am that it is entirely contrary to the spirit of the gospel, for its ministers to enter upon it from interested motives, or with great worldly expectations. On the contrary the commission is a sufficient call to them to venture all, and, like the primitive Christians, go everywhere preaching the gospel.[28]

This quote communicates the heavy sacrifice that missionaries must often make and the suffering they will likely undergo. But for those called to the work, or considering it, such a quote can make a powerful impact.

Another helpful story to cite or summarize as an illustration is the account of the Haystack Prayer Meeting. In the summer of 1806, several dedicated young men attending the Williams College in Williamstown, Massachusetts, began to gather regularly to pray and read reports of the burgeoning work of Andrew Fuller, William Carey, and the new Baptist Missionary Society in England. On one occasion, while meeting in a field adjacent to the college campus, the students got trapped by a thunderstorm, so they took shelter in a haystack. The "Haystack Prayer Meeting" resulted in the dedication of these young men to personal participation in the global missions task, and the ensuing years saw a formal American participation with the sending of Adoniram and Ann Judson and several others to the East. Recognizing the significance of that 1806 prayer meeting, later missions supporters dedicated in 1867 the Haystack Prayer Monument on the grounds of Williams College. The monument reads, "The Field is the World. The Birthplace of American Foreign Missions."[29]

The selection of the phrase "The Field is the World" is an intriguing one, but not unique given the time and missionary context. Here we find another instructive phrase to relay or reference in a sermon—or perhaps even a text around which to build an entire missions sermon. Taken from Matthew 13:38 and the Lord Jesus' explanation of the parable of the weeds, the correlation of the harvest field to the world appears first as merely background information—a description of the stage on which the parable would take place. However, as many would rightly note, the acknowledgment that the boundaries for the proclamation of the gospel are global is good and significant news for all dwellers in time and space distant from the land of Israel in the era of the New Testament. What follows is an example of how Gardiner Spring (1785–1873), a missions-minded preacher, interpreted and applied Matthew 13 in his 1840 sermon "The Extent of the Missionary Enterprise."[30]

He preached,

When our Lord proclaimed, "The field is the world," he did not mean that all the seed of the kingdom should be collected into a single furrow, or all the labor of his servants devoted to any one enclosure. When he told his followers that they were the light of the world, and the salt of the earth, he instructed them that their influence ought to be widely diffused. So when he gave the command to his church, to disciple all nations, to preach the gospel to every creature, it was not that they might confine their instruction to a few favored spots and leave the rest of the world a moral desert; nor was it that any one portion of the earth should in this respect be distinguished above another, except so far as the most effectual distribution of the gospel throughout the world might require, and his providence lead the way. . . .

We live, my brethren, for the conversion of the world. What an object! The glory of our God, the extension and adornment of his church, the welfare of our fellow men—nay, all those objects which make their appeal to the most enlarged and disinterested love of the Christian mind are embodied here. This is the object the church needs, to foster her graces, to sustain her activity, to annihilate her divisions, to give harmony and effect to her councils, and to fit her for heaven.[31]

Referencing a missions sermon of the past, like this one that God used greatly, can add weight and historic connectedness to missions sermons of the present.

Further, there is value in recounting examples of how God has used preaching on missions to call out missionaries. An often overlooked part of the life story of Adoniram Judson is that it was a sermon that compelled him to overseas service.[32] Judson's reading of Brainerd and awareness of Carey prepared him to respond to a sermon he read in September 1809 by Claudius Buchanan, at the time he needed most to hear a word from God.

Buchanan, an Anglican chaplain and friend of Carey, titled his sermon "The Star in the East" and started by citing Matthew 2:2: "For we saw his star when it rose and have come to worship him."[33] Taking the account of Jesus' birth, Buchanan inventively emphasized the uniqueness of the Gentile visitors, the wise men following a star, as "representatives of the whole heathen world." The star's eastern location, Buchanan noted, is significant because "millions of the human race inhabit that portion of the globe." Therefore, just as in the day of the arrival of God's Son, the East once again was bearing witness to the Messiah, "not indeed by the shining of a Star, but by affording luminous evidence of the divine origin of the Christian Faith." Buchanan then proceeded to speak of the spread of Christianity in the East and the need for men to take the gospel to that region of the world. Judson said that reading Buchanan's sermon enabled him to finally "break the strong attachment I felt to home and country, and to endure the thought of abandoning all my wonted pursuits and animating prospects."[34] Buchanan's sermon, which Judson acknowledged was not "peculiarly excellent" in terms of its right handling of the text, still had an epoch-making impact on his life.

A final example of how a pastor can promote missions from the pulpit is by encouraging his congregation to read books and biographies on missions. One powerful illustration of this comes from the life and death of famed missionary Jim Elliot.

As you likely know, just over sixty years ago Elliot and his four co-laborers, Ed McCully, Roger Youderian, Pete Fleming, and Nate Saint, were martyred in Ecuador. *The Shadow of the Almighty*, an account of Elliot's life and testimony written by his widow, Elisabeth, begins with these famous words:

> When Jim was a college student in 1949 he wrote these words: *"He is no fool who gives what he cannot keep to gain what he cannot lose."*
>
> Seven years later, on a hot Sunday afternoon, far from the dormitory room where those lines were written, he and four other young men were finishing a dinner of baked beans and carrotsticks. They sat together on a strip of white sand on the Curaray River, deep in Ecuador's rain forest, waiting for the arrival of a group of men whom they loved, but had never met—savage

Stone Age killers, known to all the world now as Aucas. . . .

Before four-thirty that afternoon the quiet waters of the Curaray flowed over the bodies of the five comrades, slain by the men they had come to win for Christ, whose banner they had borne. The world called it a nightmare of tragedy. The world did not recognize the truth of the second clause in Jim Elliott's credo: "He is no fool who gives what he cannot keep to gain what he cannot lose."[35]

The story of the death of the five missionaries was reported worldwide in the January 30, 1956, issue of *Life* magazine ("'Go Ye and Preach the Gospel'—Five Do and Die") and this, combined with several other publications, served as a catalyst for the gospel deployment of a generation.[36]

Interestingly, just four days before Jim Elliot would record his famous credo, he wrote in his journal about "the value of Christian biography."[37] Reading the diary of David Brainerd and other missionary biographies, Elliot said it reminded him of the counsel of Hebrews 13:7 to remember those who spoke the Word of God and to "consider the outcome of their way of life, and imitate their faith." Elliot would go on to imitate powerful faith, and it cost him his life. And others, inspired by Elliot, would go on to imitate him.

The pastor can faithfully be a missionary as a natural part of his primary duties of prayer and the ministry of the Word. He can do this by leading the congregation to pray and remember the peoples of the earth whom they know and the many whom they do not yet know. Further, by recounting in his prayer and preaching the lives and words of those who have gone before, the pastor joins a long tradition of using those means to call and strengthen missionaries. These are not additional tasks toward the pastor's ever-changing job description. Rather, they are the primary way the pastor can serve as a missionary while shepherding the flock among him (1 Peter 5:2).

The gospel-centered pastor is, by default, a missionary. He who, like William Carey, keeps the grand end in view before his congregation will therefore, like Abraham, one day see all the nations and peoples blessed (Gal. 3:8).

Pastor as Leader

— *Ronnie W. Floyd* —

I was raised in the great state of Texas. I remember sitting with my family many years ago watching Western movies. We would see cowboys taking care of their cattle on a ranch. At times, they would take a hot branding iron and press it on the skin of the calf. This would create an identifying mark on the animal. Its owner created this unique mark so that he would always know the calf belonged to him. This helped the rancher know that if the calf was ever mixed in with another herd or got separated from his livestock, he could easily find and reclaim it. This is called *branding*.

Of course, today most people don't think of animals when they hear the word *branding*. They think of business and marketing. Corporate branding is big in today's world. Companies, churches, universities, ministries, and private businesses each have a brand. Millions of dollars are invested to help create a brand or increase branding in the marketplace.

But what does it mean for a pastor to have a brand, and how does it influence his leadership?

A brand is a logo. A brand is a tagline. A brand brings distinction to who you are and what you are about. It is your sign of ownership. It is your trademark, oftentimes expressed through a graphic or tagline. We may think of branding as a superficial marketing ploy, but I'm referring to something deeper. It shows who you are and how you live.

The apostle Paul was influential because he was a branded man. Paul did not have a marketing firm that would get on social media and promote him. He had much more. Paul was a branded man because he was transformed by the power of Jesus Christ. He did not belong to himself, but to God.

How does a pastor lead as a branded man? How does the branding of the gospel shape his priorities, and how do those priorities determine his conduct? A branded pastor upholds the truth of the gospel, which bears greatly on his conduct as a leader.

The Battle for Truth

Before Paul was changed by the power of Jesus Christ, he was a passionate defender of Judaism. In fact, he was a member of a militant group in the first century that killed born-again believers. But then Paul himself was born again—branded internally by the Holy Spirit—and this changed him fundamentally.

Almost overnight Paul went from being one of the greatest opponents of the gospel to one of its greatest proponents. Paul believed wholeheartedly in the truth and power of the gospel. He believed that Christ died, was buried, and was raised from the dead on the third day. He believed eternal salvation was received when a person repented from their sin and placed their faith in Jesus Christ and Him alone. He believed this was the only way a person was declared righteous before God.

Therefore, when Paul watched false teachers—whether Judaizers or pagans—lead people astray, he felt compelled not just to *expose* their heretical teachings, but also to *expel* them, for they were undermining the gospel of Jesus Christ. He was adamant about the purity of the gospel, because he knew that to compromise its purity would empty it of power.

When you are a passionate proponent of the gospel, your theological persuasions will collide with another's. This is why Paul faced such adversity. Since the Judaizers could not change Paul's mind, they not only undermined the gospel truth but also his integrity. When Paul wrote the letter to the Christians and churches in the region of Galatia, he defended two basic things: the gospel and his calling as an apostle of Jesus Christ. In order to defend the gospel, Paul also had to defend his ministry. It was all in service to the gospel.

Thus you can understand Paul's writings partly as a battle for truth—not just the truth of the gospel, but also the truth about who he was and what he believed in so deeply. This is why he wrote in Galatians 6:14–15,

> But as for me, I will never boast about anything except the cross of our Lord Jesus Christ. The world has been crucified to me through the cross, and I to the world. For both circumcision and uncircumcision mean nothing; what matters instead is a new creation. (HCSB)

This is drastic language—and fittingly so—because Paul was a drastically changed man.

After Paul had poured out his soul defending the gospel and

his apostleship, he pointed his readers to the words above. Just as a pastor would close his message with conviction and passion, bearing his heart before his people, Paul poured out his soul through this letter. It was as if Paul was saying, "I'm going to pull the drapes back here and let you see right into my soul. This is who I am! The Judaizers can think, write, or say anything they want about me, but nothing defines me but the cross of Jesus Christ."

It was inconceivable to Paul that anyone would think he was committed to anything other than the pure gospel. As the Judaizers continued to buy into their system of belief, Paul denounced their systems and beliefs as dead. He courageously declared that they couldn't stipulate that circumcision—or anything else besides faith in Christ—was necessary for salvation. Grace is enough. Faith in Christ alone is enough. It doesn't matter whether you are circumcised or not—what matters is this: Have you ever experienced the new birth? Have you placed all of your faith in Christ alone for your salvation? What a message! This was Paul's message. This is our message.

The message was costly for Paul, and it will be costly for us. In Galatians 6:17, Paul says, "From now on let no one cause me trouble, for *I bear on my body the marks of Jesus.*" When words fail Paul in proving his commitment to the gospel, he points to his body. In essence he says, "If the marks on my body do not show that I believe in what I've been telling you I believe, then who am I? I carry the marks and the scars of Jesus Christ. He is the One who died, was buried, and was raised again for me!" What a declaration! What a message!

Paul was tired of detractors and was not giving ear to them any longer. He carried the marks of Jesus on his body, showing that he had paid a price to walk with God. His body was branded. He was a branded man. He had been persecuted for his faith in Jesus Christ. Acts 14 records his persecution in Lystra. The Scripture says he was stoned with rocks, dragged out of the city, and left for dead. Acts 16 tells us they put him in stocks and chains and beat him horribly.

The apostle Paul was branded outwardly for Jesus Christ. He used this illustratively because he saw himself as a slave of Jesus Christ. In his day and time, slaves had a brand to show who owned them. Paul was saying to them, and to all of us in this world, "Brothers and sisters, here are my marks! Jesus owns me, and I live for Jesus! Say and do what you want. I belong to Jesus."

This is a needed message for every pastor today. Pastors are not defined only by what they say or by what they preach. They are defined by what they do.

Sometimes you may think you are someone that you really are not. You cannot let a degree define you. Many have degrees. You cannot let your charisma, appearance, or apparel define you. Many have charisma, a good appearance, and fine clothing. You cannot let other people and what they say about you define you. If you do, you will live a long and miserable life. As a pastor who works constantly with people, you will become paranoid!

Pastor, what defines you? Is it the gospel of Christ? Do you bear His marks? Would all know by witnessing your life and conduct that you belong to Him? You stand behind a pulpit on Sundays to uphold the truth, but do you uphold it with your life Monday through Saturday? By now you know that the call to pastoral ministry is a weighty one. I want to encourage you with several practices that can help you bear its weight. What follows is a brief list of practices you would be wise to uphold. If you do, I believe you will soon find that the practices are actually upholding you.

Seven Practices for Every Pastor

1. Give your mornings to God

When I was a very young, full-time pastor in the state of Texas, still working on obtaining my degrees, I would always attend the powerful evangelism conference convened annually by the Baptist General Convention. Thousands attended these annual conferences, filling large convention centers in Texas.

One year, Dr. W. A. Criswell preached the final message of the evening. Criswell was the long-term pastor of the First Baptist Church in Dallas. With the Reunion Arena in Dallas filled to capacity, he called for all pastors to begin to give their mornings to God.

At that time in my life, to the best I can remember, I had just completed my master's degree and was waiting for acceptance into the doctoral program. I got on my knees that night in the convention center and made a commitment to give my mornings to God. I began the journey the next morning. On the days I was working, this commitment was to be in devotion, prayer, and study from the early morning until my first appointment at noon.

This has not been easy, but it has been a discipline I have never regretted, and by God's grace it is one I still fulfill to this day—excepting emergencies, funerals, or crucial speaking engagements.

Whether you pastor seventy-five people a week or seventy-five hundred, your most important meetings are with God each morning. You lead out of your personal walk with Christ. You preach out of your personal walk with God. There are too many preachers that have all the points down and provide glowing stories, but when they preach, there is no life at all. Do you want the touch of God on your life daily? Then commune each day with God, and when possible let it be your mornings.

We cannot overestimate the importance of God's presence in our lives. In Exodus 33:15–16, we read,

"If Your presence does not go," Moses responded to Him, "don't make us go up from here. How will it be known that I and Your people have found favor in Your sight unless You go with us? I and Your people will be distinguished by this from all the other people on the face of the earth." (HCSB)

Moses had the touch of God upon his life. He wanted to be distinguished from others by the powerful presence of God upon him. Anything less than this—your appearance, apparel, giftedness, smile, or charisma—is way less than what God wants. He wants you to be enveloped in His presence, showing forth His glory to the world. *Your personal walk with God will determine everything else in your life and ministry.*

Nothing goes further in the life of the pastor than the brand of the gospel beaming through his life due to Jesus' presence. Powerful is the filling and anointing that comes when we commune with God passionately, intimately, and daily.

2. Let God promote you

When I was a freshman in college, I was unsure about what I was going to do during the coming summer months. I became busy trying to make some things work. Then one afternoon when I was praying about it in my dorm room, the Holy Spirit spoke to me through Psalm 75:6–7. It says, "Exaltation does not come from the east, the west, or the desert, for God is the Judge: He brings down one and exalts another" (HCSB).

On that day, I began trusting God to promote me rather than

trusting myself. Each pastor wrestles daily with ego. We struggle with the desire to make sure we promote ourselves for recognition or personal gain. Anytime a pastor lives and leads this way, it leads to a dead-end street. God hates pride—absolutely detests it.

I remember one night in 1995 when I was having a hard time falling asleep. I knew God wanted me to get up and listen to Him. While fighting it initially, just before midnight I got up out of bed and went and lay on the floor with an open Bible, praying and pleading with God to speak to me.

I thought God had me up to talk to me about my church, so I began to cry out to God for my church. But then something interesting and convicting occurred. I sensed God showing me that the biggest problem with my church was not with the people but with me. I was proud and egotistical. I was an arrogant man, and I needed to get right with God.

> *When pride walks on the platform, God walks off.*

That morning, the Holy Spirit worked on me drastically, and quite honestly, that was one of the most life-changing moments I have ever experienced. The Holy Spirit showed me something that morning that I wrote in my prayer book. I've never forgotten it, and it is one of the major takeaways of that entire encounter with God: when pride walks on the platform, God walks off. Pastor, whatever your role is in the local church or ministry you serve, beware of your own pride.

3. Refuse to sacrifice your family on the altar of ministry success

We should always be thankful for growth in our churches. It is a result of God's powerful work, and He has called us to steward whatever growth He gives. Yet pastoring during times of growth comes with many challenges.

I remember one time, early in my ministry, when our church was in a particularly fruitful season. I was still quite young and had limited experience, and learning leadership in a larger church was difficult. The explosive growth of the church numerically began resulting in multiple meetings with deacons and committees as we worked together toward the future of the church. The church was very structured, so this became very demanding.

I'll never forget one day, when our boys were still pre-schoolers, I was hurrying home to see them for a brief time, and then I had to go back to the church that evening for a major meeting that I knew was going to be very challenging.

God convicted me on my way home that day. I was sitting at a stop sign—a stop sign I saw daily. But this time it held my attention, and I just gazed it. I felt like the Lord was telling me, "Stop!" The message was about my life and the way I was living and leading, sacrificing my family continually. God put these words in my heart, and I have thought of them often over the years: "Ronnie, stop sacrificing your family on the altar of ministry success."

Jeana and I celebrated forty years of marriage at the end of 2016, and I shudder to think what may have happened if I had ignored that stop sign.

The drive home that day changed my perspective greatly and brought significant change to my life, family, and ministry. God wants us to have a wonderful work ethic. Laziness in the life of a pastor is impermissible. This is not about neglecting your responsibilities. In fact, it's about fulfilling them, and your most important responsibility in ministry is your family.

As a minister of the gospel, you should never let your family be pushed aside or ignored, especially over the drive to have ministry success. At the same time, work diligently and passionately to do what needs to be done. Be wise about what you must do, should do, or can do. There are times when everyone has to make sacrifices for the sake of the whole. But these seasons come and go, and they should be the exception. There is no excuse for sacrificing your family in favor of ministry success.

Within weeks of the stop-sign incident, I began taking every Friday away from the office to spend time with my family. All of these years, I have been faithful to this commitment and rarely violate it. Today, I thank and praise God that both of my boys, their families, and my wife live passionately for Jesus, and that our relationship together is strong. Jeana and I celebrated forty years of marriage at the end of 2016, and I shudder to think what may have happened if I had ignored that stop sign.

Every pastor needs to do all he can to ensure his family loves Jesus and the church and is living out their faith individually and collectively, which creates a lasting brand that people will never forget. So let me say it again: brother and pastor, never sacrifice your family on the altar of ministry success. Prioritize and cherish your family.

4. Don't forfeit your leadership by dying on the wrong hill

As pastors, we can get into trouble when we choose to die on the wrong hills. When we do this, we lose not just sleep, but also our brand. Our testimony can become questionable among God's people. The greatest leadership lesson I have ever learned is that not every hill is worth dying on. There are definitely hills that we must be willing to die on, hills where we do not give one inch. Some of those include key doctrines like the authority of Scripture, morals that violate Christ's teaching, and ethics that harm our testimony. There are others, but these are some of the bigger hills where we need to stake our flag.

Dying on secondary hills is unwise. When you die on every hill, when you have to be right or feel you must have the last word on everything continually, you are setting yourself up to forfeit your leadership. You can forfeit your leadership in any ministry, family, or relationship when you die on the wrong hills. Gospel-branded leaders do not do this. They lead high and forward. They do what is right, not what makes them feel good or appear as if they always win. *Leadership is not about having the last word.* It's about doing what's right. Do not forfeit your leadership by fighting the wrong battles.

5. Never let anyone outside of your circle of love

Someone taught me this principle years ago, and I cannot overemphasize how important it has been in my life. Each of us has an emotional backpack full of stuff. Many pastors—whether they preach, lead musical worship, or minister in some other way—carry a pack full of disappointment, discouragement, anger, and more. They enter church to do their job, but their backpack is full. Therefore, their filling and anointing from the Spirit is quenched or grieved.

Can you relate? What is your backpack full of today? Unforgiveness? Bitterness? Criticism? Skepticism? Pastor, whatever it is, let it go.

Whether you were hurt in a devastating way in the past or there is a slow drip continuing today, drop the weight. You cannot love your flock and remain embittered against them—even if it's toward just one lamb that God has put under your care. Seek God's forgiveness and deal with whatever issues you need to in relation to yourself. Work toward reconciliation with others where you need to, and resolve never to let anyone outside of your circle of love. It doesn't matter who disapproves of your leadership or doesn't like you. It doesn't matter what someone has said or written about you. Let it go. Never do anything less than show the highest respect to God and to others. Never let anyone outside of your circle of love.

6. Always be willing to go anywhere at any time to do anything God wants you to do

When the calling of God is on your life, you release your will in choosing your geographical setting. God has called you to obey and to follow His plan that He, as the Sovereign One, is dictating to you. Remember that we are not branded by anyone other than the Lord Himself. We are not branded by our church, seminary, denomination, or ministry, and those entities do not dictate how God uses us.

God determines where you are and where you go in your life. I share this with pastors everywhere, and I am committed to live and lead this out personally: live like you will be where you are for the rest of your life, but at the same time, live with your bags packed and ready to go. Be willing to go wherever and whenever God wants you to go. Simultaneously, be willing to stay where you are. There are times in ministry where going is easier than staying. Since we are branded by Jesus and belong only to Him, He is the leader of our lives and ministries. He determines where we go on the map. Our role is to follow Him. Therefore, always be willing to go anywhere at any time to do anything God wants you to do. Whether it's a geographical move or something more difficult, let the marks on Paul's back be a constant reminder to you that you are not above your Master. Carry whatever cross He gives you.

7. Remember that God can do more in a moment than you can in a lifetime

Pastor, recapture your deep belief in, and commitment to, the power of God in your ministry. If you wonder if God can use you, the answer is yes. God can do more in a moment than you can in a lifetime.

We live in a church culture today that is not necessarily friendly to the power of God, but God is alive as ever. He is the same God who birthed you supernaturally by causing you to be born again, and He is the same God who can wake up a dead church. Yes, our God can even take the most boring preacher and make him a spiritual giant in the pulpit. He can strengthen you to lead with courage. He can bring growth to your church. Do not underestimate the power of God, but rather plead for it and endeavor to depend on it fully.

We need the power of God in life and ministry. I need the power of God in my life and ministry. I pray for the day when the power of God defines us. May we all live and lead believing that God can do more in a moment than we can in a lifetime.

Pastor, you are branded by something much greater than you— the gospel of Jesus Christ, the power of God unto salvation (see Rom. 1:16). Does your life proclaim that? These simple leadership lessons I've provided are just the start. Go beyond them. Let these and any other godly principles undergird your life and ministry so that you might more faithfully bear the name of Christ. If you lead like He wants you to, sooner or later you will wear His marks on your back. When these trials come, you'll be glad to have laid a solid foundation for your ministry and leadership. Woe to the leader who meets trial without the strength of God.

Pastor as Man of God

— *Donald S. Whitney* —

N ot every man of God is a pastor, but every pastor must be a man of God.

Men who serve in parachurch ministries, as denominational employees, as church staff members, and even as Christian lay leaders should be men of God. But God does not call all men of God to be pastors. He calls all pastors to be men of God—without exception.

Godliness is to the pastor what flight is to the eagle. Without personal godliness, the wings of pastoral ministry are broken. Thus personal holiness—that is, Christlikeness, sanctification, godliness—should be the primary pursuit of every pastor.

Unconverted doctors, lawyers, athletes, and tradesmen can ignore the pursuit of godliness and still enjoy the favor of men and unbounded success in their earthly endeavors. But if a pastor ever ceases to be a man of God, he forfeits God's favor on his labors and any true fruitfulness in his ministry. A pastor may not necessarily be effective in organization, insightful in financial matters, or skillful in staff leadership—though it's much better for him if he is—but he must be a godly man.

The Man of God in Scripture

The term "man of God" appears seventy-eight times in the English Standard Version of the Bible. All but two uses of the term are in the Old Testament. Five men in Scripture are mentioned by name as men of God. Specifically, there are six references to "Moses the man of God." Three times the designation "David the man of God" appears. Elisha and Shemaiah are identified by name as men of God twice each, and once we read of "Hanan the son of Igdaliah, the man of God." Although the term rarely appears adjacent to its referent, in almost all cases in the Old Testament the identity of the man of God is clear. For example, when the servant of the future King Saul says to him, "Behold, there is a man of God in this city" (1 Sam. 9:6), he is obviously referring to the prophet Samuel. When in 1 Kings 17:24 the mother of the boy who has just been raised from the dead says, "Now I know that you are a man of God," she is speaking to the prophet Elijah.[1]

An examination of the seventy-six uses of "man of God" in the Old Testament reveals the following points.

A man of God is chosen by God

Famous are the episodes in which God appeared to Moses in the burning bush, called to Samuel in the night, chose David above his brothers, and instructed Elijah to anoint Elisha. These men were divinely appointed, not self-selected. Today, no real pastor becomes a pastor simply by pronouncing himself one—God must call him. By means of what has historically been referred to as the "internal call" of the Holy Spirit, combined with the "external call" of a church that formally recognizes the hand of God upon a man in accordance with the qualifications of 1 Timothy 3, God chooses the pastor.[2]

A man of God represents God

For these Old Testament figures, the title "man of God" became their identity. For many of them, the term became synonymous with their name, as with "Moses the man of God." With some it replaced their name, so that "man of God" is the only personal designation we have for them in the Bible. In each case, the "man of God" was God's man—a man so identified with God that he was to be a type of ambassador or representative of God. The same should be true for every pastor of every New Testament church, as the apostle Paul indicates in 2 Timothy 3:17 when he uses the term "man of God" for a pastor. A pastor is God's man for leading the church; therefore, he must be a godly man. The office of pastor does not make him a holy man; he must be a holy man to hold the office.

A man of God speaks with God

The biblical record makes clear that men of God both heard from God and prayed to God. The Lord spoke to Moses, as Caleb reminded Joshua: "You know what the LORD said to Moses the man of God in Kadesh-barnea concerning you and me" (Josh. 14:6). As a man of God, Moses prayed to God, as indicated in the inspired title of Psalm 90, "A Prayer of Moses, the man of God." We find elsewhere this two-way communication between God and His men when we read that "the word of God came to Shemaiah the man of God" (1 Kings 12:22) and that "the man of God entreated the LORD" (1 Kings 13:6). It is no less important for those of us who shepherd God's flock today to be men in communion with God. Getting alone with God to learn what He has said to the world through His Word—the Bible—and to "devote ourselves to prayer" as the apostles did (Acts 6:4) remain top priorities for men of God in every age and culture.

A man of God speaks for God

The most sacred responsibility of a man of God has always been to speak for God—that is, to relay to others the message he has received from the Lord for them. In the Old Testament, we repeatedly encounter language such as that found in 1 Samuel 2:27, "And there came a man of God to Eli and said to him, 'Thus says the LORD . . . ,'" and in 1 Kings 20:28, "And a man of God came near and said to the king of Israel, 'Thus says the LORD . . .'" In the New Testament, the apostle Paul, as he came to the climax of his instructions to Timothy about pastoral ministry, solemnly exhorted him—a man he specifically addressed in 1 Timothy 6:11 as a "man of God"—to "preach the word" (2 Tim. 4:2). Above all else, Timothy's pastoral calling was to speak for God—that is, to publicly proclaim God's words, the Scriptures. The same holy duty and privilege presses upon all pastors in all times and all places.

Jesus Christ is the ultimate man of God

The embodiment of each of these roles was the perfect man of God, Jesus Christ. He was the chosen one of God—the uniquely Anointed One—sent as the Messiah to save God's people. He was the preeminent representative of God in the world, the very Son of God, who came on behalf of the Father. He spoke with God in the most intimate communion possible, for as He said of Himself, "I and the Father are one" (John 10:30). As the perfect prophet of God whose every word was the Word of God, He spoke for God. "What I say," Jesus declared in John 12:50, "I say as the Father has told me."

Jesus, therefore, is the ultimate reference point for all subsequent men of God. He is the standard by which they must now be measured. He is the example to which they must now seek to conform, however imperfectly. He is the goal to which they must now point. He is the message they must now proclaim.

"Man of God" in the New Testament refers to pastors

So when we think of "man of God" today, we must first think of Jesus. But as mentioned above, of the seventy-eight occurrences of "man of God" in Scripture, two of them are specifically reserved for use in the New Testament. All the meanings of the Old Testament term "man of God" not only continue in the two New Testament uses of it, but also reappear with even greater strength. Significantly, in both instances (1 Tim. 6:11 and 2 Tim. 3:17) the term refers to a pastor.

The first is 1 Timothy 6:11: "But as for you, O man of God, flee these things. Pursue righteousness, godliness, faith, love, steadfastness, gentleness." This text mandates specific character requirements for a pastor, something not found in any Old Testament passage about a man of God. Moreover, most of these qualities are primarily New Testament emphases, and some (like faith, love, and gentleness) also appear in Galatians 5:22–23 as particular evidences or fruit of the Holy Spirit's work in a believer. These imply that a man of God today is, above all else, a man who knows Jesus Christ, not simply someone with the title "pastor." By the power of the Holy Spirit, who helps him "flee" the vices mentioned in verses 7–10 and "pursue" the qualities listed in verse 11, the man of God is growing in Christlikeness. And although these characteristics are not objectively measureable, they are observable. Thus, the man of God's growth in Christlike graces is evident to the people of God whom he shepherds.

Here in 1 Timothy 6:11, Paul directly addresses Timothy as a man of God, though by implication the title applies to every faithful pastor, as does every part of the epistle. But the other New Testament use of the term is clearly addressed to all pastors, not just to Timothy. For in 2 Timothy 3:16–17 we read, "All Scripture is breathed out by God and profitable for teaching, for reproof, for correction, and for training in righteousness, that the man of God may be complete, equipped for every good work." Every man of God moves toward "completion" (that is, Christlike maturity) as a pastor and receives the necessary equipment for every good work in ministry from a Book "breathed out by God." To be a man of God means to be a man of God's Book. A pastor ought to live in and by the Bible so much so that through it the Holy Spirit constantly teaches, reproves, corrects, and trains him.

Now that we have examined how Scripture describes a man of God, we can explore further why a pastor must be one.

Why Should the Pastor Be a Man of God?

To ask why a pastor should be a man of God is similar to asking why a brain surgeon should be intelligent; it is essential to the nature of the work. As it is fundamental to the task that a jockey be small and light, that a combat soldier be gritty and courageous, that an author be literate, so a pastor must be godly.

God's command for pastors

For starters, a pastor should be a man of God because God explicitly commands it. God expects the shepherds of His flock to be men of God. The Lord inspired the apostle Paul to write to Pastor Timothy—and thereby to all pastors—"Keep a close watch on yourself and on the teaching. Persist in this" (1 Tim. 4:16). In other words, "Watch your life and doctrine closely" (NIV). A life of personal holiness for a pastor is placed on the same level of importance with something as crucial as sound doctrine.

Notice also that the pastor is to "persist in this" (v. 16). That is, he should persist in keeping a close watch on his life and doctrine to his last breath. Regardless of his age, spiritual maturity, experience, or education, no pastor ever reaches a level of spirituality where he can stop growing in holiness and commitment to sound doctrine. No man of God even wants to.

The clear will of God for every man of God is that he engage in a constant, disciplined, blood-earnest pursuit of growth in both heart and head, spirit and truth, heat and light, and piety and theology until he sees Jesus. Any pastor not resolved to do this can question whether he has been called to the ministry at all.

In his *Lectures to My Students*, Charles Spurgeon reminded his ministerial protégés, "True and genuine piety is necessary as the first indispensable requisite; whatever 'call' a man may pretend to have, if he has not been called to holiness, he certainly has not been called to the ministry."[3] So to speak of a "holy pastor" should be considered as redundant as "wet water." Conversely, an "unholy minister" is as much a contradiction in terms as "dry water."

The pastor's work is the work of God. Therefore, he must be a man of God. A minister is set apart by the church and recognized by others as a representative of Christ. But if the man is a living contradiction to Christ, he cannot represent Christ. Moreover, the church does not want such a man—unless, of course, the church is filled with worldly people. Worldly people do not want a godly leader. They want someone like themselves. The true people of God, however, long for a genuine man of God to be their shepherd, someone whose life is an example of what a follower of Jesus ought to be.

"Examples to the flock"

That is why the apostle Peter exhorts all pastors to be "examples to the flock" (1 Peter 5:3). Pastors may wonder, *Examples of what, exactly?* Ultimately, this means they should be Christlike examples in every area of life. Ministers must model godliness to God's flock, providing them with a pattern of holiness they can see and follow. Yes, God primarily calls pastors to preach His Word to His people, for by this means they will understand God's truth about holiness. But the pastor should also model by his life and piety how to apply God's truth about holiness in everyday life. The pastor's calling involves not only teaching Christians from Scripture how to live as Christians, but also showing them by his example.

The pastor must be a man of God because he cannot lead the members of the church to a life of godliness he himself does not know or experience. He cannot guide them on paths of spiritual maturity that he has not traveled. He cannot show the way to holiness if he does not know the way. His ministry will not be a means to produce godly people if he is not a godly man.

The longer a pastor serves a church, the more it tends to reflect both his strengths and weaknesses. If his heart is ablaze with ardor for God above all else, his heart fire will stir the embers of others. But if his spirituality smolders, the hearts of his people will grow cold. If Jesus is central in his preaching and his life, the church will be increasingly enamored with Christ's beauty. But if the pastor minimizes Christ in his ministry, they will likely be "looking to Jesus" (Heb. 12:2) less and less. If he depends on the power of the Holy Spirit, his people are more likely to do so. But if he relies less on the Holy Spirit and more on his education, experience, and eloquence, his church will grow dull in its sensitivity to the Spirit's presence and power. If the pastor manifests a love for and submission to the Word of God, his people will cherish the Scriptures also. But if the sound of Scripture becomes less prominent in his sermons and conversation, the ears of the church members will begin to itch, and they will grow less interested in biblical truth. If his prayers in the pulpit reveal the soul of a man who also prays in private, his church will become more of a praying church. But if his prayers are dry and professional, he will deaden the prayer lives of his people. If a pastor witnesses to the lost in the community—and his people will know if he does—and has a passion for the nations, the members of the church will develop a burden for the lost. But if he demonstrates little initiative in sharing the gospel, his people will demonstrate none. If he lives and gives as though his treasure is in heaven, his people will give to the Lord sacrificially. But if he is not a cheerful and generous giver to the Lord's work, his people will see giving as a routine duty, detached from gospel joy.

The church will never rise spiritually above the level of its leadership. A people will never become godlier than their pastor. The pastor is the pacesetter; that's what it means to be an example. When Paul says to Pastor Timothy, "Set the believers an example in speech, in conduct, in love, in faith, in purity" (1 Tim. 4:12), he is indicating that pastors must show the church what Christlikeness looks like here and now. Christians should get their cues of what God-honoring speech is from their pastor. They will know what Christlike conduct is by watching his conduct. He should strive to be the most like Jesus "in love, in faith, in purity" and in all Christlike qualities so that they will see how they need to grow in them. Whatever the pastor wants his people to live out, he must do it the most.

When he exhorts his people to godliness, he must be able to speak of intimacy with Christ as a witness, not merely as an advocate. A witness speaks with the credibility and passion of experience. An advocate can speak truth but seem detached, like someone fulfilling a role. Sometimes a mere advocate can even preach with passion about godliness, but it sounds like a half-sincere, temporary, cultivated zeal.

It takes a man who walks with God to show others how to walk with God. If he does not provide a witness and an example, his church will become, at best, like the church at Sardis, of which Jesus said, "You have the reputation of being alive, but you are dead" (Rev. 3:1). The Christlikeness of a congregation will never outpace its pacesetter.

How Can the Pastor Most Faithfully Be a Man of God?

Only God can make a man of God. Godliness—and growth in it—is always and only a result of God's grace. Any attempt to produce godliness by human effort alone is legalism or the dead work of the flesh.

But growing as a man of God is not a matter of passive waiting, either. If that were God's plan, we would certainly have a passage somewhere in the Pastoral Epistles similar to the command of Jesus to the apostles just before Pentecost, when "he ordered them not to depart from Jerusalem, but to wait for the promise of the

Father" (Acts 1:4). Instead, in the Pastoral Epistles we find imperatives like "train yourself for godliness" (1 Tim. 4:7). Explicit instructions like this make it clear that growth in godliness requires effort—grace-initiated, grace-empowered, persistent, lifelong, and disciplined effort. The desire and power for both godliness and its means—namely, biblical spiritual disciplines—must come from God, but their daily practice must be done by the man of God.

Flee sin and pursue holiness

The best places for a New Testament pastor to learn how to most faithfully be a man of God would obviously be those New Testament passages written to pastors where they are specifically described as men of God. So we return first to 1 Timothy 6:11—"But as for you, O man of God, flee these things. Pursue righteousness, godliness, faith, love, steadfastness, gentleness."

As mentioned earlier, this text teaches that pastoral godliness consists in part by fleeing certain things—namely the myriad of sins found in verses 3–10—and pursuing others, in this case the Christlike qualities found in the rest of verse 11 as well as those found in the three imperatives of verses 12–14. Space does not allow for even a brief exegesis of these two paragraphs (that is, vv. 3–14), so permit me to summarize by saying that a practical, everyday part of a pastor's life involves bolting from sin and running hard after holiness.

This is more than saying that a man of God should avoid sin in general. Rather, this passage presents godliness in terms of fleeing specific sins. A faithful man of God identifies particular sins in his life, such as conceit, envy, slander, and evil suspicions (see v. 4), and takes action against such sins by name. He knows, for example, that he is sometimes tempted to envy another pastor's ministry or the financial prosperity of some of his church members, and when those temptations rear their head, he turns from them and runs toward contentment. Perhaps he runs to particular thought patterns that always help him embrace contentment.

But being a man of God is much more than sin avoidance; it also involves cultivating specific fruits of righteousness. For instance, he may be keenly conscious of his need for more steadfastness or gentleness (see v. 11). This is typically because of his too-frequent thoughts of leaving his place of ministry and his impatience with the inability of others to keep up with his pace. He strategizes how to facilitate sensitivity and growth in these qualities, perhaps including others who can counsel him on making progress.

However he does it, the point is that the man of God is intentional and specific about fleeing sin and pursuing holiness. It is not just a general war against sin and love of godliness; he is conscious of particular battles and certain habits.

Become a Bible-controlled man

An unbreakable bond between godliness and the Bible is proclaimed in the other New Testament text that uses the term "man of God" in reference to a pastor: "All Scripture is breathed out by God and profitable for teaching, for reproof, for correction, and for training in righteousness, that the man of God may be complete, equipped for every good work" (2 Tim. 3:16–17). These verses show that to remain faithful as a man of God, a pastor must be a Bible-controlled man. By means of ongoing absorption of the God-breathed Book, he is continually taught, reproved, corrected, trained, and equipped by it.

Jesus Himself prayed essentially the same for His disciples—and for all "who will believe in [Him]" (John 17:20)—when He prayed that they would be made holy by the Word of God. He asked the Father, "Sanctify them in the truth; your word is truth" (John 17:17).

There is only one way to be a Bible-controlled, truth-sanctified man of God: devotion to the disciplines of the Word.[4] These include *hearing* the Bible read and preached,[5] *reading* through it regularly to know and remember all that it says, *studying* it deeply to the end of your days, *memorizing* it to keep its treasures within you, *meditating* on it to experience God through it, and *applying* it to be a continually transformed doer of the Word.

In my ministry experience, meditation on Scripture is the single greatest devotional need for most Christians, including pastors. The distractions produced by technological progress make meditation increasingly difficult, but perhaps no discipline of the Word is more catalytic to growing in the others. Reading is the exposure to Scripture—and that is the starting place. But meditation is the absorption of Scripture, and it is the absorption of Scripture that leads to intimacy with God and the life transformation we long for when we come to Scripture.

Through reading, we receive the indispensable truth of Scripture, but through meditation we *experience* the truth of Scripture. Through reading, for example, we learn that "God is love" (1 John 4:8), but through meditation we feel the love of God—we experience "a felt Christ," as the Puritans were known to say. Of course, we do this in biblically appropriate ways, not unduly mystifying the knowledge of Christ, but knowing Him in spirit and in *truth*. Knowing God's truth is first, foundational, and foremost, but knowing the truth without experiencing it and being affected by it is a heartless, clinical Christianity. I urge every Christian—including every pastor—to build time for meditation on the Word of God into their daily Bible intake. No man is a Bible-controlled man who fails to think deeply and often about what God has said.

Practice the disciplines of godliness

The inspired command, "Train yourself for godliness," was first written to a pastor (Timothy, the "man of God") in 1 Timothy 4:7. The practical ways Christians live out this exhortation to train or "discipline"[6] themselves are often called "spiritual disciplines." By spiritual disciplines I mean those "personal and interpersonal activities given by God in the Bible as the sufficient means believers in Jesus Christ are to use in the Spirit-filled, gospel-driven pursuit of godliness, that is, closeness to Christ and conformity to Christ."[7]

No pastor should operate under the illusion that other Christians must practice the spiritual disciplines to grow in godliness but that he himself will become more Christlike by virtue of being in the ministry. Apart from a life of practicing the God-given means of experiencing God and growing in holiness, the ministry will actually become the means of making a man more *un*godly. The routines of ministry will eventually anesthetize him to the holiness of his work, much as they did to some of the Old Testament priests whose regular temple rituals simply became their jobs, callousing their hearts to the holy things of God they handled every day. The temptations a pastor will face in terms of discouragement, money, sex, power, pride, and cynicism will eventually bring him down without the grace God gives only through the personal and interpersonal spiritual disciplines found in Scripture.

Let me emphasize it again: Paul was inspired to write "train yourself for godliness" first to a pastor. No pastor can faithfully remain a man of God apart from the biblical disciplines we practice both individually and corporately within the church. There are experiences with God and His grace that are unique to the personal spiritual disciplines as well as to the interpersonal ones. A pastor needs to be alone with God just as Jesus needed it. In the church, a pastor needs to be the lead worshiper, not just the worship leader. A pastor should not just fence the Lord's Table, he should also feast his soul on Christ there. As much as any other Christian, but also as an example to other Christians, a pastor should practice the disciplines of godliness.

I want to conclude by asking two very serious questions.

First, do you recognize the intentionality necessary to cultivate and sustain godliness in ministry? No man coasts into Christlikeness, not even a man who serves Christ full-time in vocational ministry. Neither does anyone become a more faithful man of God by accident. No man grows in godliness who does not intend to. More than intentionality is needed, but unless a pastor deliberately pursues holiness, he will suffer the spiritual decline and the ministry-destroying effects caused by the gravity of worldliness.

Do not assume you are a man of God just because you are in the ministry. No ordination or office transforms a worldly man into a man of God. A church can choose you as its pastor, but no church process can make you a true man of God. No title transmits holiness. Godliness is not something pronounced upon you; it's something you must pursue.

Do not assume you are a man of God because you used to be a man of God. There are countless ministerial casualties involving men who entered the pastorate with spiritual zeal. As the years passed, their spiritual devotion was more frequently sacrificed on the altar of the demands of the ministry. The resulting barrenness of busyness began to erode their holiness until the day when their life and ministry collapsed—becoming yet another casualty of the sinkhole syndrome.

What Hebrews 12:14 commands every Christian is equally binding for pastors: "Strive . . . for the holiness without which no one will see the Lord." A man may serve in ministry for fifty years and preach thousands of sermons, but according to this verse, if he does not "strive" for holiness, he will not see the Lord. Striving for holiness does not qualify us for heaven. Only the holiness of Jesus deserves heaven, and we will enter heaven by trusting in His righteousness, not our own. Nevertheless, it is true that without striving for holiness "no one will see the Lord," because those who fail to strive for holiness prove that they do not know the Holy One and are not indwelled by the Holy Spirit. But my point at this juncture is that striving for holiness does not happen unintentionally. You do not "train yourself for godliness" (1 Tim. 4:7) without deliberateness. You do not "keep a close watch on yourself" (1 Tim. 4:16) as an afterthought.

Second, will you resolve to make the pursuit of pastoral holiness a top priority? The first priority of a man of God is to be a godly man. There may not be many men of God in your church, but there better be at least one. If you will not make the pursuit of God and godliness a priority, it is better to leave the ministry than to remain in it as a contradiction to all that a minister of Christ is supposed to be.

A man of God knows he has to *make* time for the means of godliness. That is what you do with your actual—as opposed to professed—priorities. If a man is indeed a man of God, the Holy Spirit will give him a desire for godliness, but the man himself must make a priority of the means of godliness. Since the work of ministry is never done—there will always be more sermon prep to do and more people to visit or counsel, etc.—you cannot wait until you have time to pray and to meditate on Scripture, for you will never have time. You cannot become a man of God in your spare time. A man of God does not push the pursuit of godliness to the edges of his life; it *is* his life. To faithfully do the work of God, you must make a priority of being a man of God.

The godly nineteenth-century Scottish pastor Robert Murray M'Cheyne put it this way: "It is not great talents God blesses so much as great likeness to Jesus."[8] Similarly, Richard Baxter, the Puritan pastor extraordinaire, said this concerning pastoral holiness: "Take heed to yourselves, for the success of all your labors doth very much depend upon this."[9]

A pastor must be a multifaceted man: preacher, shepherd, evangelist, counselor, leader, theologian, visionary, organizer, manager, and more. But if he is not a man of God, he cannot expect the blessing of God upon any of these roles. Have you sought to be something else more than a man of God? Perhaps you have longed more to be a visionary than a man of God. Maybe you hope to be regarded as having a clever mind more than a godly life. Possibly you have worked harder to cultivate a persona of coolness than Christlikeness. Does it mean more to you to be known as a hard worker than as a holy man?

Christian author Os Guinness quoted a Japanese businessman who said, "Whenever I meet a Buddhist leader, I meet a holy man. Whenever I meet a Christian leader, I meet a manager."[10] Every Christian minister will face a lifelong temptation to decline into a mere religious manager or anything other than a holy man. Nevertheless, despite all you must do as pastor, you must first and foremost be a man of God.

Conclusion

— *Jason K. Allen* —

Teddy Roosevelt, the twenty-sixth president of the United States, is considered one of the greatest elected officials in our nation's history and one of the greatest leaders the world has ever known. He was a tsunami of energy—one who never saw a mountain too tall to scale or a fight too threatening to join. He shook the nation, invented the modern presidency, and left a changed country in his wake. There is a reason why his face, along with the faces of Washington, Jefferson, and Lincoln, is chiseled on Mount Rushmore.

Roosevelt, reflecting on the burden of leadership and the willingness to risk all and attempt great things, famously observed,

> It is not the critic who counts, not the man who points out where the strong stumbled, or how the doer could have done better. The credit belongs to the man who is in the arena, his face marred by dust and sweat and blood, who strives valiantly, who errs, and falls short again and again: There is no effort without error.

But he who tries, who knows the great enthusiasms, the great devotions, who spends himself in a worthy cause, at best knows the triumph of achievement, and at the worst, fails while daring. His place shall never be with those cold and timid souls who know neither victory nor defeat.[1]

Every time I read Roosevelt's quote, my mind darts to the pastorate and to the fine work that men of God do. The office of the pastorate is a high one, the work is a noble one, and the men who faithfully undertake it are worthy of our admiration. This book's purpose has been to help you toward this end. You are in the arena, putting your life on the line. My challenge to you is to press on.

As you press on, and as you process and incorporate the contents of this book, let me encourage you, one last time, about who you are in Christ, the stewardship He has entrusted to you, and the uniqueness of your ministry.

First, you are called by God. Christ has given the church, in our age, "evangelists, and some as pastors and teachers, for the equipping of the saints for the work of service, to the building up of the body of Christ" (Eph. 4:11–12 NASB). One does not stroll into the ministry; one surrenders to it, receiving it as a weighty gift and calling. Pastors are those who have been set apart by God, who are called by His Spirit, and who have submitted their lives to Him. This requires obedience not only to enter the ministry, but to continue in it. So celebrate the calling, and in your submission to it, press on.

Second, you are a minister of the Word. Your one irreducible responsibility is to feed the sheep the Word of God. Paul stipulates that the pastor "must be . . . able to teach," and he charged Timothy to "give attention to the public reading of Scripture, to exhortation and teaching," and to "preach the word" (1 Tim. 3:2; 4:13; 2 Tim. 4:2 NASB). The pastor who faithfully discharges this responsibility does more than explain the Bible, he feeds the church—eternal souls—the bread of the eternal Word. Every Christian needs a steady intake of God's Word, and a faithful pastor who rightly divides the Word weekly is worthy of high praise. In your ability to handle the Word, press on.

Third, you are held to a higher level of accountability. The task of preaching and the responsibility of spiritual accountability bring a higher level of accountability upon you. It begins with the qualifications of the office, as outlined in 1 Timothy 3:1–7 and Titus 1:6–9, but it extends to other passages as well. For example, James 3:1 cautions the church, "Let not many of you become teachers, my brethren, knowing that as such we will incur a stricter judgment" (NASB). Hebrews 13:17 declares that leaders keep watch over their flock "as those who will give an account" (NASB). These qualifications are all the more daunting when you realize that pastors face more intense temptation. Satan targets those whose fall will do the most damage to the church and most sully God's glory. Therefore, live a sober, Spirit-led life. In your fitness for ministry, press on.

Fourth, you confront more intense temptation. Peter tells us that Satan roams about as a roaring lion seeking those whom he may devour; and there is no one he enjoys devouring more than a Christian minister—especially an erstwhile faithful one (1 Peter 5:8). When he does, he not only ruins a pastor and his ministry, he also destroys a family, disrupts a church, and discredits God's glory in that community. There simply is no sin like the sin of a clergyman, and there is no one Satan desires to bring down more than the one whom God is using most fruitfully. Guard your heart. In your battle against temptation, press on.

Fifth, you face unique pressures. There are days pastors carry the weight of the world, and for reasons of confidentiality, all they can do is bottle it up. Whether it is a piercing word of criticism, a church member's scandalous sin, a draining counseling session, a rigorous day of sermon preparation, or just the operational challenges of most congregations, all of these burdens—and more—can mount up to make the strains of ministry seem at times nearly unbearable. In these times, stay firmly grounded in Christ and seek your strength in His faithfulness. In your dependence on God, press on.

Sixth, you tend the flock of God. Pastors are more than a shoulder to cry on, and they offer more than consolation during life's trials. They preach, lead, and fulfill a host of other responsibilities, but pastors are men who are willing to bear their congregants' burdens of heart. When church members need prayer, counsel, or support, pastors stand in the gap for them. They bear these burdens with their flocks. Paul spoke of his affection and parental care of the believers in Thessalonica, and Peter exhorted the elders to shepherd the flock with eagerness, not lording it over them. Such is the heart of a pastor: one who loves his congregation. This is no easy task. Church members can be wayward, stubborn, and even rebellious. Thus, the pastor who loves and serves the flock is worthy of admiration. In your care for the sheep, press on.

Pastor, this is you. This is your calling, your work, and your reward. The point of this book is not to raise the bar of ministry unapproachably high, but to give you the encouragement and counsel to most faithfully serve the body of Christ. As you do, you will honor God, strengthen His church, and one day hear, "Well done, my good and faithful servant." So press on.

Notes

Pastor as Shepherd

1. *Christianity Today* editorial, "What *Reveal* Reveals," *Christianity Today*, February 27, 2008, http://www.christianitytoday.com/ct/2008/march/11.27.html.

2. Greg L. Hawkins and Cally Parkinson, *REVEAL: Where Are You?* (South Barrington, IL: Willow Creek Association, 2007), 65.

3. Jonathan Edwards, "Farewell Sermon," in *The Works of President Edwards with a Memoir of His Life* (New York: S. Converse, 1829), 1:641, 644–45.

4. D. A. Carson, *The Gospel According to John* (Grand Rapids: Eerdmans, 1991), 676–78.

5. John Calvin, *John*, Crossway Classic Commentaries (Wheaton, IL: Crossway, 1994), 467.

6. Edward Mote, "My Hope Is Built on Nothing Less" (1834).

Pastor as Husband and Father

1. Lance Morrow, "Men: Are They Really That Bad?," *Time*, February 14, 1994, http://content.time.com/time/magazine/article/0,9171,980115,00.html.

2. Weldon Hardenbrook, "Where's Dad? A Call for Fathers with the Spirit of Elijah," in *Recovering Biblical Manhood and Womanhood: A Response to Evangelical Feminism*, ed. John Piper and Wayne Grudem, redesign ed. (Wheaton, IL: Crossway, 2012), 378.

3. "The Extent of Fatherlessness," National Center for Fathering, http://www.fathers.com/statistics-and-research/the-extent-of-fatherlessness/.

4. Abigail Wood, "The Trouble with Dad," *Seventeen*, October 1985, 38.

5. John Croyle, "Four Things Every Parent Should Know," *Focus on the Family Magazine*, May 1996, 2.

6. Barbara Kantrowitz and Claudia Kalb, "Building a Better Boy," *Newsweek*, May 11, 1998, 58.

7. "Pie Chart," *Time*, June 30, 1997, 22.

Pastor as Preacher

1. Martyn Lloyd-Jones, *Preaching and Preachers* (Grand Rapids: Zondervan, 1971), 9.

2. Ibid., 26.

3. R. Albert Mohler Jr., *He Is Not Silent* (Chicago: Moody Publishers, 2008), 50.

4. Alistair Begg, *Preaching for God's Glory* (Wheaton, IL: Crossway, 1999), 23.

5. Haddon W. Robinson, *Biblical Preaching: The Development and Delivery of Expository Messages* (Grand Rapids: Baker, 1980), 21.

6. Bryan Chapell, *Christ-Centered Preaching: Redeeming the Expository Sermon* (Grand Rapids: Baker Academic, 2005), 131.

7. Hershael York and Bert Decker, *Preaching with Bold Assurance: A Solid and Enduring Approach to Engaging Exposition* (Nashville: B&H, 2003), 11.

8. John Broadus, *On the Preparation and Delivery of Sermons* (San Francisco: HarperCollins, 1979), 3–7.

Pastor as Theologian

1. For more context, see Kevin J. Vanhoozer and Owen Strachan, *The Pastor as Public Theologian: Reclaiming a Lost Vision* (Grand Rapids: Baker, 2015); E. Brooks Holifield, *God's Ambassadors: A History of the Christian Clergy in America* (Grand Rapids: Eerdmans, 2007). A personal account of such ministry can be found in John Piper and D. A. Carson, *The Pastor as Scholar and the Scholar as Pastor: Reflections on Life and Ministry*, ed. Owen Strachan and David Mathis (Wheaton, IL: Crossway, 2011).

2. John Stott, *Guard the Gospel: The Message of 2 Timothy* (Downers Grove, IL: InterVarsity, 1973), 60.

3. For more on training boys to be godly men, see Owen Strachan and Gavin Peacock, *The Grand Design: Male and Female He Made Them* (Fearn, Scotland: Christian Focus, 2016).

4. For one powerful account of this recovery, see Paul Pressler, *A Hill on Which to Die: One Southern Baptist's Journey* (Nashville: Broadman & Holman, 1999).

5. Gordon Fee, *1 and 2 Timothy, Titus* (Grand Rapids: Baker, 1988), 180.

6. To better understand the gospel, consult these works: Steve Jeffrey, Mike Ovey, and Jeffrey Sach, *Pierced for Our Transgressions: Rediscovering the Glory of Penal Substitution* (Wheaton, IL: Crossway, 2007); John Murray, *Redemption Accomplished and Applied* (1955; repr., Grand Rapids: Eerdmans, 2015); Jared Wilson, *The Pastor's Justification: Applying the Work of Christ in Your Life and Ministry* (Wheaton, IL: Crossway, 2013).

7. John Calvin, *Institutes of the Christian Religion*, 2:1156–57 (4.8.9), quoted in Vanhoozer and Strachan, *Pastor as Public Theologian*, 78.

8. Charles Spurgeon, "The Form of Sound Words," in *The New Park Street Pulpit*, vol. 2 (1856; repr. Pasadena, TX: Pilgrim Publications, 1975).

9. Thomas Oden, *First and Second Timothy and Titus* (1989; repr., Louisville, KY: John Knox Press, 2012), 131.

10. For more on the call to ministry, see Jason K. Allen, *Discerning Your Call to Ministry: How to Know For Sure and What to Do About It* (Chicago: Moody, 2016); C. H. Spurgeon, "The Call to the Ministry," in *Lectures to My Students: A Selection from Addresses Delivered to the Students of the Pastors' College, Metropolitan Tabernacle*, Lectures to My Students 1 (London: Passmore and Alabaster, 1875), 18–39.

11. See Alister McGrath, *Luther's Theology of the Cross: Martin Luther's Theological Breakthrough* (London: Wiley Blackwell, 1991). This biblical concept—found in Matthew 16:24 and Luke 9:23, among other texts—can scarcely be surpassed as foundational for pastoral ministry and the Christian life beyond it.

12. For more on this kind of ministry, see Mark Dever and Jamie Dunlop, *The Compelling Community: Where God's Power Makes a Church Attractive* (Wheaton, IL: Crossway, 2015).

13. Matthew Henry, "Commentary on 2 Timothy 1," in *Matthew Henry's Commentary on the Whole Bible*, ed. George Burder and John Hughes (1811), http://st-takla.org/bible/commentary/en/nt/matthew-henry/timothy2/ch1.html.

14. For more on how to ground Christians in the biblical worldview, see Owen Strachan, *The Colson Way: Loving Your Neighbor and Living with Faith in a Hostile World* (Nashville: Thomas Nelson, 2015).

15. For more on how pastors may speak to the theological concerns of their context, see Gerald Hiestand and Todd Wilson, *The Pastor Theologian: Resurrecting an Ancient Vision* (Grand Rapids: Zondervan, 2015).

16. Iain Murray and J. C. Ryle, *Prepared to Stand Alone* (Edinburgh: Banner of Truth, 2016), 194.

17. For more on these crucial but often-underplayed matters, see Peter Gentry and Stephen Wellum, *God's Kingdom through God's Covenant* (Wheaton, IL: Crossway, 2015).

18. Quoted in Vanhoozer and Strachan, *Pastor as Public Theologian*, 83. See Jonathan Edwards, "Pastor and People Must Look to God," in *The Salvation of Souls: Nine Previously Unpublished Sermons on the Call to Ministry and the Gospel*, ed. Richard Bailey and Gregory Wills (Wheaton, IL: Crossway, 2012), 142. For more on Edwards's life and ministry, see Owen Strachan and Douglas Sweeney, *The Essential Edwards Collection* (Chicago: Moody, 2010), which consists of five short books: *Jonathan Edwards: Lover of God*; *Jonathan Edwards on Beauty*; *Jonathan Edwards on the Good Life*; *Jonathan Edwards on True Christianity*; *Jonathan Edwards on Heaven and Hell*.

Pastor as Church Historian

1. Augustine, *Civ. Dei*, 18.51.2, in *The City of God in The Works of Aurelius Augustine, Bishop of Hippo: A New Translation*, trans. Marcus Dods (Edinburgh: T&T Clark, 1871), 2:285–86.

2. Charles Spurgeon, *The Metropolitan Tabernacle Pulpit: Sermons Preached and Revised by C. H. Spurgeon during the Year 1863* (Pasadena, TX: Pilgrim Publications, 1969), 9:668, italics in the original.

3. Charles Spurgeon, *Charles H. Spurgeon's Autobiography, Compiled from His Diary, Letters, and Records, by His Wife, and His Private Secretary*, vol. 3, *1856–1878* (London: Passmore and Alabaster, 1899), 43.

4. J. B. Cranfill, comp., *Sermons and Life Sketch of B. H. Carroll* (Philadelphia: American Baptist Publication Society, 1895), 42.

5. Carl F. H. Henry, *God Who Speaks and Shows*, vol. 1, *Preliminary Considerations in God, Revelation and Authority* (1976; repr., Wheaton, IL: Crossway, 1999), 30.

Pastor as Evangelist

1. Art Toalston, "Southern Baptists Need 'A Long-Term Vision of Great Commission Advance,'" *SBC Life* (Summer 2016): 2. If we work from those same numbers, it takes fifty-two SBC church members to reach a single person with the gospel.

2. Minutes of the St. Joseph Baptist Association's *2016 Annual Report*, St. Joseph, MO. Meeting held and minutes approved on September 18, 2016.

3. The word translated "go" is an aorist participle in the Greek text. The presence of the participle has led some to translate it this way: "As you are going, make disciples." The stronger evidence, though, falls on the side of seeing the use of the aorist participle combined with the imperative to create a command of necessity (see Matt. 2:8; 9:13; 11:4; 17:27; and 28:7 for the same structure). Daniel Wallace calls this a verb of attendant circumstance. The participle carries the same force as the main imperative since it is necessary to accomplish the participle to fulfill the main command. Daniel Wallace, "The Great Commission or the Great Suggestion?," February 17, 2014, https://danielbwallace.com/2014/02/17/the-great-commission-or-the-great-suggestion/.

4. These challenges are clearly delineated from vv. 16–42 and include legal action against them, flogging, betrayal by family, hatred directed toward them, overt persecution, and even death.

5. Michael Green, *Evangelism in the Early Church* (Grand Rapids: Eerdmans, 2003), 17.

6. Ibid., 24.

7. Larry Norman, "I Wish We'd All Been Ready," on *Upon This Rock*, Capitol Records, 1969, compact disc. More recently the song has been covered by DC Talk and later by Jordin Sparks.

8. Rodney Stark, *The Rise of Christianity: How the Obscure, Marginal Jesus Movement Became the Dominant Religious Force in the Western World in a Few Centuries* (San Francisco: Harper San Francisco, 1997), 14, 20.

9. Ibid., 20.

10. Charles Spurgeon, "Golden Bowls Full of Incense," in *The Metropolitan Tabernacle Pulpit*, vol. 18 (Carlisle, PA: Banner of Truth, 1976).

Pastor as Missionary

1. John Fountain, "From Mr. Fountain to Mr. Fuller," in Eustace Carey, *Memoir of William Carey, D.D.* (London: Jackson and Walford, 1836), 286, italics added. For a brief introduction to Carey, see Jason G. Duesing, *Seven Summits in Church History* (Wake Forest, NC: Rainer Publishing, 2016).

2. Rich Mullins and David Beaker Strasser, "Sometimes By Step," on *Songs*, Reunion Records, 1996, compact disc. Lyrics available at https://www.kid brothers.net/lyrics/sbs.html.

3. John Piper, *Let the Nations Be Glad! The Supremacy of God in Missions*, 3rd ed. (Grand Rapids: Baker, 2010), 191–92, explains, "What we may conclude from the wording of Genesis 12:3 and its use in the New Testament is that God's purpose for the world is that the blessing of Abraham, namely, the salvation achieved through Jesus Christ, the seed of Abraham, would reach to all ethnic groups of the world. This would happen as people in each group put their faith in Christ and thus become 'sons of Abraham' (Gal. 3:7) and heirs of the promise (Gal. 3:29). This event of individual salvation as persons trust Christ will happen among 'all the nations.'"

4. John Piper, *Brothers, We Are Not Professionals: A Plea to Pastors for Radical Ministry* (Nashville: B&H, 2013), 223.

5. Ibid.

6. This paragraph is adapted from my forthcoming entry in the *Worldview Study Bible* (Nashville: B&H, 2018).

7. Piper, *Brothers*, 223.

8. This paragraph is adapted from Jason G. Duesing, "A Plea for Ambitious Evangelicals," in *Union University Pulpit* (2013): 43–51.

9. Piper, *Let the Nations Be Glad!*, 217.

10. Zane Pratt, M. David Sills, and Jeff K. Walters, *Introduction to Global Missions* (Nashville: B&H, 2014), 27–30.

11. Robin D. Hadaway, "A Course Correction in Missions: Rethinking the Two-Percent Threshold," *SWJT* 57, no. 1 (Fall 2014).

12. In fact, Pratt, Sills, and Walters, *Introduction to Global Missions*, 27–30, argue that for greatest accuracy, the term *unreached* needs further refinement into "unengaged unreached people groups" (UUPGs) and "uncontacted unreached people groups" (UUUPGs). The UUPGs are groups whose population is less than 2 percent evangelical; who are hidden, hostile, or isolated; among whom no church planting has taken place for the last two years; and with whom no contact has ever been made for the advancement of the gospel.

13. Ibid., 30.

14. Danthemankhan, "40 Window world map," *Wikipedia*, uploaded July 19, 2006, https://commons.wikimedia.org/wiki/File%3A40_Window_world_map.PNG.

15. Pratt, Sills, and Walters, *Introduction to Global Missions*, 32.

16. Tom Stellar, "Afterword," in Piper, *Let the Nations Be Glad!*, 264.

17. Robert E. Speer, "What Constitutes a Missionary Call?" (Student Volunteer Movement for Foreign Missions, 1923), http://www.thetravelingteam.org/articles/a-missionary-call.

18. "Status of World Evangelization 2017," Joshua Project, February 2017, http://joshuaproject.net/assets/media/handouts/status-of-world-evangelization.pdf.

19. "World Watch List," Open Doors, https://www.opendoorsusa.org/Christian-persecution/world-watch-list/.

20. Executive Committee of the Southern Baptist Convention, "Annual of the 2016 Southern Baptist Confession," St. Louis, MO, June 14–15, 2016, http://www.sbcec.org/bor/2016 /2016SBCAnnual.pdf. In addition to a mismatch of sent personnel, there is also the mismatch of resources. In my own missions-focused denomination, the Southern Baptist Convention, for example, in 2014–2015 the 46,793 churches reported total resources of $11.5 billion. Of that number, a total of $227 million was reported as money designated to fund global missions. While that is an astounding number, and reflective of a heart for the peoples of the world, it remains only 2 percent of our total resources.

21. C. S. Lewis, *The Voyage of the Dawn Treader* (1952; repr., New York: Harper-Collins, 1998), 225.

22. Jonathan Edwards, *An Humble Attempt*. (Boston: D. Henchman, 1747) in Stephen J. Stein, ed., The Works of Jonathan Edwards, vol. 5, Apocalyptic Writings, (New Haven, CT: Yale University Press, 1977), 308–437. This section is adapted from my forthcoming entry in *The Jonathan Edwards Encyclopedia* (Grand Rapids: Eerdmans, 2017).

23. Michael J. McClymond and Gerald R. McDermott, *The Theology of Jonathan Edwards* (New York: Oxford University Press, 2011), 565.

24. Joseph A. Conforti, *Jonathan Edwards, Religious Tradition, and American Culture* (Chapel Hill: University of North Carolina Press, 1995), 75. For more on Edwards, see an expanded version of this paragraph in Duesing, *Seven Summits*.

25. Allison Meier, "How an Imaginary Island Stayed on Maps for Five Centuries," *Hyperallergic*, September 20, 2016, http://hyperallergic.com/316836/how-an-imaginary-island-stayed-on-maps-for-five-centuries/.

26. Jason Mandryk, *Operation World* (Downers Grove, IL: InterVarsity, 2010). For more information, see http://www.operationworld.org/.

27. W. O. Carver, professor of comparative religion and missions at Southern Baptist Theological Seminary, wrote in reflection on the life of pioneer mis-

sionary Adoniram Judson that Judson's life had an effect "not only in drawing men into service, but rather more, perhaps, in sustaining men in service." See Carver, "The Significance of Adoniram Judson," *Baptist Review and Expositor* 10 (October 1913): 478.

28. William Carey, *An Enquiry into the Obligations of Christians to Use Means for the Conversion of the Heathens* (1792), http://www.wmcarey.edu/carey/enquiry/anenquiry.pdf.

29. For more on the "Haystack Prayer Meeting," see Jason G. Duesing, "More than a Needle Found: 'The Field is the World' Proclaimed from a Haystack," *Footnotes* (blog), September 10, 2013, http://jgduesing.com/2013/09/10/more-than-a-needle-found-the-field-is-the-world/.

30. "Obituary, Rev. Gardiner Spring, D.D.," *New York Times*, August 20, 1873, http://query.nytimes.com/mem/archive-free/pdf?res=9F02E2DD143FE23BBC4851DFBE668388669FDE. See also Gardiner Spring, *Missionary Paper, No. XXI: The Extent of the Missionary Enterprize* (Boston: Crocker and Brewster, 1840), https://ecommons.cornell.edu/bitstream/handle/1813/29836/Z168_11_0592.pdf;sequence=1.

31. Spring, "Extent of the Missionary Enterprise."

32. This section is adapted from Jason G. Duesing, "For Judson, a Sermon Pointed Him Eastward," *Baptist Press*, October 2, 2012, http://www.bpnews.net/38833/for-judson-a-sermon-pointed-him-eastward; and Jason G. Duesing, "Breaking the Strong Attachment to Home and Country: The Influence of a Friend of Fuller's Friends on Adoniram Judson," *Southern Baptist Journal of Missions and Evangelism* 1, no. 2 (Fall 2012): 6–13.

33. Claudius Buchanan, *The Star in the East* (New York: Williams & Whiting, 1809). For further context for this and other sermons by Buchanan, see Karen Chancey, "The Star in the East: The Controversy over Christian Missions to India, 1805–1813," *Historian* (March 1998).

34. Adoniram Judson to Stephen Chapin, December 18, 1837, quoted in Francis Wayland, *A Memoir of the Life and Labors of the Rev. Adoniram Judson, D.D.* (Boston: Phillips, Sampson, and Company, 1853), 1:51–52.

35. Elisabeth Elliot, *Shadow of the Almighty* (New York: Harper & Row, 1958), 15, 19.

36. "'Go Ye and Preach the Gospel'—Five Do and Die," *Life*, January 30, 1956, 10–18.

37. Elisabeth Elliot, *Shadow of the Almighty: The Life and Testament of Jim Elliot* (Grand Rapids: Zondervan, 2009), 108.

Pastor as Man of God

1. In an unusual use of the term, each of the parents of Samson refers to an angel as a "man of God" (Judg. 13:6, 8). In verse 6 Samson's mother "told her husband, 'A man of God came to me, and his appearance was like the

appearance of the angel of God, very awesome.'" Though she says the one who came to her had an angelic, "very awesome" appearance, perhaps she (and later her husband) spoke of him as a "man of God" because he also possessed very definite human (and evidently male) characteristics. Similarly, when the women came to the tomb of Jesus early on the morning of His resurrection, they encountered an angel inside, but Mark describes him as "a young man sitting on the right side, dressed in a white robe" (Mark 16:5).

2. The "internal call" to pastor is derived from the language of 1 Timothy 3:1, which speaks of a man who "aspires" for and "desires" the "office of overseer." Then the local church, not the pastoral candidate, determines whether the man possesses the qualities found in verses 2–7, qualities that a pastor "must" (a term used four times in this brief section) have. For more on the call to pastoral ministry, see Jason K. Allen, *Discerning Your Call to Ministry* (Chicago: Moody, 2016).

3. Charles H. Spurgeon, *Lectures to My Students* (1881; repr., Pasadena, TX: Pilgrim Publications, 1990), 1:3.

4. In chapters 2 and 3 of Donald S. Whitney and J. I. Packer, *Spiritual Disciplines for the Christian Life*, rev. and updated ed. (Colorado Springs, CO: NavPress, 2014), I go into detail about the disciplines of hearing, reading, studying, meditating on, memorizing, and applying the Word of God.

5. Even pastors who preach to others on a frequent basis will themselves profit from hearing others preach the Word.

6. Some translations, such as the New American Standard Bible, render this as "discipline yourself for the purpose of godliness."

7. Whitney and Packer, *Spiritual Disciplines*, 9.

8. Andrew A. Bonar, *Memoir and Remains of the Reverend Robert Murray M'Cheyne* (Edinburgh: Oliphant, Anderson and Ferrier, 1894), 239.

9. Richard Baxter, *The Reformed Pastor* (1656; repr., Edinburgh: Banner of Truth, 1974), 80.

10. Os Guinness, *Dining with the Devil* (Grand Rapids: Baker, 1993), 49.

Conclusion

1. Brian M. Thomsen, ed., *The Man in the Arena: Selected Writings of Theodore Roosevelt; A Reader* (New York: Forge, 2003), 5.

Acknowledgments

A t least to some degree, every book is a joint effort—especially this one. First, I am grateful for my colleagues who chose to join this project. These men are all good friends, gifted leaders, faithful ministers, and accomplished scholars. These contributors not only made this book better, they made it possible.

At the personal level, every project I undertake depends on the support, prayers, and encouragement of my family. God has abundantly blessed me with a wife in Karen, and a family in Anne-Marie, Caroline, William, Alden, and Elizabeth, who have surpassed my every hope and dream as to what they'd be and mean to me. They are an artesian well of love, joy, support, and satisfaction. Without them, my life and ministry would be so lacking.

At the institutional level, my colleagues and office staff likewise are an invaluable source of support and encouragement. Most especially, I'm thankful for Patrick Hudson, Tyler Sykora, Dawn Philbrick, and Catherine Renfro. These men and women are an absolute delight to serve with, and the graciousness and competence with which they fulfill their responsibilities are a daily encouragement and inspiration to me.

Furthermore, I'm thankful to the team at Moody Publishers, most especially Drew Dyck and Matthew Boffey. These men, and the publisher they serve, make great partners.

Last, and most of all, I'm indebted to my Lord and Savior, Jesus Christ. Like every other ministerial undertaking, none of this would be possible without his grace, calling and gifting. May this book, and all that I do, bring him much glory, be used to strengthen his pastors and the churches they serve.